Cello Online
String Sampler

Cello Study Guide

By Robin Kay Deverich

Global Music School String Publications

Graphic Design by Julia Kay

ISBN 9780982385630

http://www.celloonline.com

TABLE OF CONTENTS

Preface

Cello Online String Sampler Study Guide explains the history, style, and musical form of the 54 cello pieces featured in the *Cello Online String Sampler Cello Sheet Music* (sold separately). This study guide provides a brief overview of the various styles, music history periods, and cultures represented in the string sampler sheet music such as Medieval, Renaissance, Baroque, Classical, Romantic, 20th Century, Fiddle, Klezmer, Gypsy, Chinese, Greek, Carnatic, Arabic, Mariachi, Ragtime and Blues. Information about the history and musical form of the selected pieces is presented, and cello technique tips are included for each piece. At the end of the guide, a music glossary and bowing chart are provided to explain additional concepts.

As an added bonus, sound files of each piece are currently available on a website, Cello Online™: *http://www.celloonline.com*   In addition to sound files, Cello Online™ content includes a review of cello basics such as instrument care and tuning; cello playing position; fingering assistance; cello technique tips; scales and etudes; and music theory basics.

Making music can bring you joy, and this string sampler is designed to help you actively learn, study and play beautiful string music from a wide variety of styles and eras. Let the music begin!

*No guarantees are made that these sound files and website will be available indefinitely.

STUDY UNIT 1—MEDIEVAL & RENAISSANCE MUSIC

MEDIEVAL & RENAISSANCE MUSIC SECTIONS

Fig. 1.1 *Angel with fiddle, c.1478-80*

SECTION 1.1

EARLY STRINGED INSTRUMENTS

When were stringed instruments first used? As early as 1700 B.C., written records and artwork document the use of early stringed instruments such as the plucked cithara used in ancient Greece, Egypt, Assyria, and Asia Minor.[1] In the early tenth century, the bowed two-stringed Arabic rabab and the bowed lyra were used throughout the Islamic and Byzantine empires,[2] and this led to the development of the bowed three-stringed rebec, patterned after the Arab rabab and the Byzantine lyra.[3]

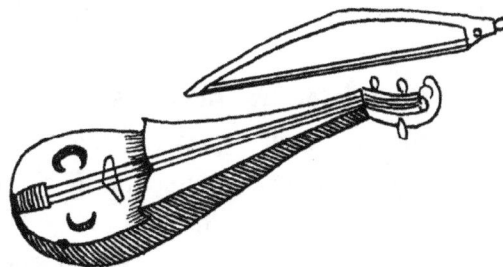

Fig. 1.2 *Rebec illustration, 1529*

Were stringed instruments such as the violin, viola and cello (often defined as the violin family) patterned after one of these early instruments? Scholars have found it difficult to determine exactly when and where members of the violin family were first created. John Dilworth noted the difficulty of tracing the origins of these instruments when he stated:

> Instruments played with a bow appear in European carvings and illustrations from around 900 AD, but interpretation is difficult, and the names given for them in texts vary and overlap. Broadly speaking, however, they fall into four categories: the rebec, the Medieval and Renaissance fiddle, the *lira da braccio* and the viol. Of these, the first three are generally accepted as ancestors of the violin and viola, because of their playing positions and sizes. . . the distillation of the various families of instrument, such as the three-stringed rebec and the seven-stringed lira, into the four-stringed violin with carved back and front, provided a form which could easily be extended to the larger sizes for the consort, the viola supplying the middle voice and the cello as the bass instrument. The full name of the instrument, the 'violoncello', did not become widely agreed until the late seventeenth century.[4][5]

SECTION 1.2

MEDIEVAL MUSICAL PERIOD OVERVIEW (450-1450)

1) **Significant role of the Christian Church.** The Medieval period of music covers a wide span of time, and many changes in music occurred during this era. The Christian Church was the primary patron of music and the arts, and most of the surviving Medieval music manuscripts we have today consist of sacred vocal music composed for religious services such as Masses.

2) **Beginnings of music notation.** Music notation first began as a tool to assist monks who had to memorize large numbers of melodies to accompany texts for religious services. Monks were the ones who notated and preserved this music called plainchant (also known as chant). Plainchant is characterized as having a monophonic texture (single melody) without a measured rhythm. Today, this music is often called Gregorian Chant in honor of Pope Gregory I (590-604) who collected and standardized plainchant. During the mid to late Medieval period, chant developed a polyphonic texture (a form of musical texture with several interdependent, overlapping melodic lines) when additional melodies were added (organum), and new sections (conductus).

3) **Rising influence of royalty and the aristocracy in secular music.** During the 12th century, members of royal courts and aristocrats began to play a rising role in music, both as patrons of the arts and as active participants in music making. Secular music included monophonic and polyphonic songs such as ballatas, caccias, rondeaus, and virelai, composed by entertainers such as golliards, jongleurs, troubadours and trouveres. Some of these musicians were traveling

entertainers and poets; others were associated with courts, including aristocrats and members of royalty, and they often sang of courtly love.

4) **Few surviving examples of instrumental music**. Although artwork and writings from the Medieval period make it clear that instrumental music was abundant, few manuscript sources of notated instrumental music have survived. Jongleurs (also called minstrels) were expected to play as many as ten instruments,[6] and some were skilled at using the fiddle to play the tenor and contratenor parts of three-voice polyphonic songs. It is likely that troubadours and trouveres also sang their songs to instrumental accompaniments or instrumental doubling of their vocal parts. Much of this instrumental music was probably improvised or passed on through oral tradition. A few pieces of instrumental dance music which have survived are called estampies and istanpitta.[7]

SECTION 1.3

MEDIEVAL MUSICAL STYLE CHARACTERISTICS

Performing Medium. During the Medieval period, music was primarily vocal. Instruments were used to accompany vocal lines or to improvise instrumental dances, and very little instrumental music has survived.

Rhythm. Rhythm was not notated during much of this period, and traditions regarding the treatment of sacred text, the meter of the text, and the musical abilities of singers and instrumentalists often determined the rhythmic complexity and tempo of pieces.

Melody. Melodic intervals and the range of melodies were generally small during this era (Hildegard of Bingen was an exception), and sacred melodies were often based on church modes (modes are notes arranged in a specific scale or pattern of intervals, and were often used to structure the melody or tonality of a piece).

Harmony. Harmony and tonality as we know it today were not functional during the Medieval period. Music appears to have been constructed and heard as separate lines rather than vertical sonorities. Parallel fifths and octaves were favored, and triads or thirds were considered dissonant.

Texture. Monophonic texture was predominantly used during the first part of this era, and polyphonic texture began to be used in the mid to late Medieval period. Heterophony may have been heard in performances.

Form. Popular genres during this period included the following large forms: sacred vocal music such as plainchant, conductus, masses, and motets; instrumental estampies, and secular vocal songs.

PIECE: COLUMBA ASPEXIT

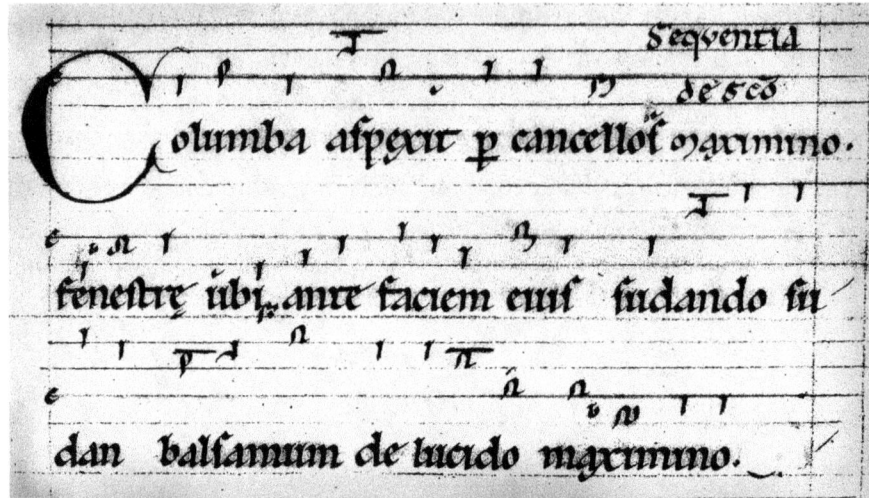

Fig. 1.3 *Columba Aspexit manuscript*

Columba aspexit was written during the Medieval Period, and was composed by Hildegard of Bingen (1098-1179), abbess of a convent in Rupertsberg, Germany (near Bingen). In addition to being a church leader, Hildegard also was a theologian, visionary, composer, and writer. Hildegard's religious writings were recognized and approved by religious authorities such as Pope Eugenius II and Saint Bernard of Clairvaux. As a result, throughout her life, many sought her counsel such as popes, emperors, religious leaders and laypeople.[8] It is interesting to note that women during the Medieval period had few rights or privileges, and other than a few notable exceptions (*e.g.* women of nobility such as Eleanor of Aquitaine or women with religious ties such as Hildegard), women did not generally occupy positions of power or influence.

Hildegard was a prolific composer, and wrote music to fill religious needs in her convent such as music for Offices, Masses and special services. Hildegard wrote *Columba Aspexit's* text and music for a special church service: a Mass honoring Saint Maximus. This piece was written in plainchant: a single melody sung by a soloist or choir. Hildegard's melody features syllabic, neumatic and melismatic passages. These terms are used to indicate that instead of each syllable of the text being sung to a single note (syllabic), some syllables call for several notes (neumatic) or many notes per syllable (melismatic). Hildegard used this technique and a soaring melody with a wide range to highlight and emphasize the descriptive imagery of her poetic text. As illustrated in the image of Hildegard's manuscript, during the Medieval period, rhythm was not notated. Musically, this is described as "free rhythm" or "unmeasured rhythm," meaning the rhythm is set by the performer. The musical form used in this piece is called a sequence: a chant of the Mass sung between sections called the Alleluia and the Gospel. In this form, each melodic phrase is generally sung twice, with a slight variation the second time: AA'BB'CC' Although Hildegard's *Columba aspexit* manuscript is notated only for voice, she apparently approved of the use of instruments with her music. She wrote in one of her books of visions: "We are to praise God with the trumpet, harp, zither, organ, drum, strings, flute, cymbals, dance."[9] Stringed instruments during the Medieval period included rebecs and Medieval fiddles, and a fiddle is shown in the image below from one of Hildegard's books of visions.

Fig. 1.4 *Heavenly Musicians, 1240*

TECHNIQUE TIPS: During Hildegard's time, if a stringed instrument such as a rebec or medieval fiddle were to play along with the vocal part of *Columba aspexit,* the instrumental part would likely have been a drone: one sustained note throughout the entire piece (an open D in this arrangement). To try this, place your bow at the frog and begin with a down-bow, playing long, smooth bow strokes on your open D as the melody line is played or sung. When you change bows, do so as smoothly as possible so your note will sound sustained and unbroken throughout the piece. While playing, you may want to watch your bow to make sure you're able to draw it in a straight line, parallel between the bridge and the fingerboard.

Although Hildegard's *Columba aspexit* melody was intended for singers, it has been included in this collection of pieces to provide an example of music from this era. Hildegard's melody features a lovely soaring melodic line that floats up and down, mirroring the expressive text with phrases that seem to call for slight pauses. Experiment with slurs and bow changes to see how you can create a smooth, flowing melody and decide when and where you feel the need to slightly pause your bow to indicate when you have reached the end of a musical phrase.

SECTION 1.5

PIECE: SIXTH ROYAL ESTAMPIE

It is likely that a vielle or rebec was used to play "Sixth Royal Estampie," an instrumental dance piece from the Medieval period. This piece came from a collection of 13th century French trouvere songs called the *Chansonnier du Roy* (The King's Songbook).[10]

Estampies are considered to be some of the oldest surviving notated versions of instrumental music.[11] The musical form of this particular piece consists of four melodic phrases which are each repeated with a first or second ending (a first ending the first time the melodic phrase is repeated, and a second ending the second time the melodic phrase is repeated). Similar first and second endings are used at the end of all four melodic phrases.

TECHNIQUE TIPS: Since this piece calls for a lively dance tempo, you may want to play it in the upper half of your bow. Some slurs may make the bowing easier, and some of the phrases should begin with an up-bow. Towards the end of the piece, a Bb accidental is used.

SECTION 1.6

RENAISSANCE MUSIC OVERVIEW (1450-1600)

1) **Renaissance—"rebirth" of ideas**. The Renaissance was a time of renewed appreciation for learning and the arts. The term renaissance, "rebirth" of ideas, reflects an interest in the principles of classical Greek and Roman culture, and this era was a time of artistic accomplishments, scientific discoveries, and exploration of new lands.

2) **Patrons of music included the Church and members of the aristocracy.** Both secular and sacred music flourished during this period. Although the Church continued to be an influential patron of the arts, the Renaissance was a time when wealthy aristocrats became avid supporters of the arts, and the sign of a well-educated gentleman or woman, was one who was proficient in music.

3) **New instruments were invented.** Instrumental music was very popular, and new instruments such as the viol and violin were created during the Renaissance. Like other melodic instruments, violins and viols were made in coordinated sets of several sizes, often called a consort or family of instruments. For performances, instruments were often grouped into loud and soft ensembles. Loud ensembles (generally for outdoor playing) consisted of converted folk instruments such as shawms, bagpipes, trumpets, pipes, and percussion. Soft ensembles (for indoor performances) were comprised of instruments such as the viol, harp, lute, recorder and

violin. Keyboard instruments such as the organ, harpsichord and clavichord were also invented during this period.

4) **Advances in music printing led to mass publication of printed music**. As music became affordable and widely available, printed music and numerous music instruction books began to be published for amateurs, and composers began writing music for amateur musicians.

SECTION 1.7

RENAISSANCE MUSICAL STYLE CHARACTERISITICS

Performing Medium. During the Renaissance era, music was primarily performed by vocal groups (ensembles of one to eight parts). When instruments were used with voices, they often performed the same lines. Instrumental music included ensembles (consort music) and solos (such as keyboard music for the organ or harpsichord).

Rhythm. As in the Medieval period, tempos were still determined by the musician as well as the sacred character of the piece or text. During the Renaissance era, rhythm began to increase in complexity, and by the end of this period, regular meters began to appear.

Melody. Melodic range increased during this era, and melodic movement generally had a smooth consonant contour, with small conjunct intervals predominating. Musical phrases were balanced, and the use of embellishing tones was carefully regulated.

Harmony. Composers sought to blend the sounds of voices and instruments during this era. The use of the Medieval period's parallel fifths and octaves were avoided, and pleasing harmonies were sought such as triads and sixths. Although dissonances were freely used in Medieval music, Renaissance music prepared and resolved any dissonances with consonant harmonies. Towards the end of the sixteenth century, modern harmonic tendencies begin to appear.

Texture. Polyphonic texture was predominately used, and music with many separate lines provided different sonorities and densities. Instead of using the Medieval period's contrasting and independent lines, efforts were made to have voices blend by having musical lines present the same musical phrase, one after another.

Form. Important genres during this period included the following large forms: motet, mass, madrigal, chanson (French for song), keyboard music, instrumental consort music and instrumental dance music.

SECTION 1.8

PIECE: HELAS MADAME

Helas Madam was composed by Henry VIII (1491-1547), King of England. Before Henry VIII became King in 1509, part of his education included training in music. Music played a prominent role in his court, and for entertainment, he played numerous instruments and composed music. The piece *Helas Madame* is found in a collection of secular music used at King Henry's court. Some scholars have noted that the melody may have originated elsewhere in continental Europe, with King Henry adding the harmony.[12] The musical form of this piece is a song with a homophonic texture and minor harmony.

TECHNIQUE TIPS: Use a lively tempo to play the melody of this piece. You may want to use slurs for some of the notes. A slur is a curved line grouping notes together, and is indicated by the sign ⌒. Notes included in the slur should be played in the same bow.

SECTION 1.9

PIECE: KEMP'S JIGG

"Kemp's Jigg" is a popular dance tune from the 16th century. The composer is unknown, but this piece is said to have been composed in honor of Will Kemp, a famous Elizabethan actor who wagered he could dance 80 miles from London to Norwich in nine days (he supposedly won the bet). During this period, the musical form of jig meant a vigorous, up and down dance. The term jigg was also used to define a popular form of entertainment: a short burlesque comedy combining music, drama and dance, performed by two to five characters who sang their lines to popular tunes, interspersed with lively dancing. Professional comedians such as Kemp participated in these jigg performances, and Kemp's Jigg is one of the well-known jigg tunes from this period.[13] [14]

TECHNIQUE TIPS: This piece has a strong, two beat pulse in each measure. Use a rollicking dance tempo throughout the piece. Dotted quarters, slurs, and short crisp bows with slight separations between the notes are just a few of the effects you could use to help maintain the momentum of this high-spirited dance.

SECTION 1.10

VIOLIN CONSORTS

Although most music historians rely on artwork to try to date when the violin and other members of the violin family were first created, Peter Holman sought to establish the date of the violin's inception by examining how the early violin was used and played. He observed that in sixteenth century art music, melodic instruments were made in coordinated sets of several sizes (often three or four sizes pitched a fourth or fifth apart), and that these families of instruments were called consorts. Holman determined that the first usage of the violin was in a consort, and he concluded that the violin family emerged between 1495-1505 in Ferrara, Italy. Violin music seems to support Holman's assertion, because the majority of violin music from the 16th and early 17th centuries appears to be for violin consorts, and it was not until the mid-17th century that solo repertoire for the violin developed.[15] It is also interesting to note that solo repertory for the cello did not emerge until the late 17th century,[16][17] and although there were a few incidents of solo music being written for the viola in the 17th century, it wasn't until the mid-18th century that solo repertory for the viola emerged.[18][19]

Figure 1.5 is an illustration of members of a violin consort, the instruments found in the violin family: violin (soprano violin), viola (alto-tenor violin) and violoncello (bass violin, also known as the cello). Another instrument, the double bass or contrabass is also often considered to be part of the violin family, but music scholars have differing views whether or not the double bass came from the violin family or the viol family, and for this reason it has not been included in this discussion.

Fig. 1.5 *Violin Family, 1619*

SECTION 1.11

PIECE: FANTASIA

Fantasia is an example of instrumental consort music, and this piece was composed by Thomas Lupo (1571-1629), a member of the English royal violin consort from 1591 until his death in 1628. One of Thomas Lupo's titles was "composer to the violins."[20] It is interesting to note that four generations of the Lupo family served as court musicians in England, beginning with Thomas's grandfather who emigrated from Italy to serve in King Henry VIII's court in 1540.[21]

Fantasia was written for a four-part instrumental consort, and may have been played by either violin or viol consorts, or possibly a mixed chamber ensemble of viols and violins.[22] The musical form of this piece is a fantasia, defined as being: "A term adopted in the Renaissance for an instrumental composition whose form and invention spring 'solely from the fantasy and skill of the author who created it' (Luis de Milan, 1535)."[23]

TECHNIQUE TIPS: *Fantasia* includes slurs, ties, accidentals and dotted quarters. Although Lupo's original music indicated the melody should be exchanged between the different instruments in the consort, this arrangement has been simplified to feature the melody in the part you are playing.

SECTION 1.12

WHO PLAYED THE VIOLIN?

Neal Zaslaw described who was likely to play the violin during its early years:

> During the first part of its meteoric career, the violin was played in public by formally trained professionals, servants, and illiterate folk musicians. Ladies and gentlemen, when entertaining themselves in private circumstances, preferred the elegant sounds of viols and lutes to the raucous power of brash fiddles. The violin appears first to have entered 'polite society' as a consort instrument.[24]

As Zaslow noted, during the 16th century, playing the violin (including other members of the violin family such as the viola and cello) was primarily regarded as a trade, and well-bred amateurs favored instruments such as the viol. David Boyden referred to the lowly status of the violin during this period when he stated:

> For the most part, reputable people and musicians in the sixteenth century thought of violins as instruments of lowly origin played mainly by professionals. In comparison, viols and lutes, both belonging to an older and more aristocratic tradition, were played not only by professionals but also by amateurs and gentlemen, who ardently admired these instruments.

To play the viol or especially the lute was considered an admissible, even highly desirable, part of the general education of the well-born; and these instruments enjoyed a vogue among persons of social standing, who as amateurs generally regarded music as a commendable avocation, but not as a proper profession. The violin enjoyed none of this social prestige.[25]

SECTION 1.13

MUSIC TUTORS FOR AMATEURS

During the 16th century, large numbers of instructional treatises for amateur musicians were published. Thurston Dart and William Coates commented on the heightened interest of amateurs in music instruction during this time period:

> By 1575 or so there was every sign of a steadily increasing public and private demand for vocal and instrumental music. London bookshops sold tutors for the lute and cittern, books of printed music paper, and collections of printed and manuscript music mainly imported from the Low Countries; musical instruments were becoming less costly, music teaching less exclusive, musical notation less abstruse.[26]

David Price offered several reasons why amateurs became so interested in music literacy and performance during this era:

> By the middle decades of the sixteenth century, and in some places even before then, the reading and writing of music had taken its place within a broadening spectrum of educational possibilities. Literate musical ability was reflected in and stimulated by literature, by travel, by the entertainment or imitation of royalty, and by social ambition. Perhaps this developing literacy was to be seen most clearly in the lives of members of the governing classes but nonetheless simpler expressions of the pleasure of reading and writing music revealed themselves among all classes of society. Indeed the growing number of musical tutors, primers and treatises suggest that a revolution in musical education accompanied that in general standards of literacy, thereby creating its own class of potential musical patrons.[27]

Examples of musical instruction for amateurs included vocal tutors such as Thomas Morley's *A Plaine and Easie Introduction* (1597), lute tutors geared for amateurs such as Adrien Le Roy's English version of *A briefe and easye instruction to learne the tableture* (1568), Sylvestri Ganassi's two-volume viol tutor: *Regola Rubertina* (Venice, 1542, 1543), and tutors designed to assist musicians with multiple instruments such as: Gasparo Zanetti's *Il scolaro...per imparar a suonare di violino, et altri stromenti* (1645, for violin, viola and cello).

Boyden commented on the popularity of tutors for musical amateurs, in particular, violin tutors which became extremely popular beginning in the seventeenth century:

> The first violin tutors were essentially 'do-it-yourself' books. Often regarded as a modern phenomenon, such books flourished during the seventeenth and eighteenth centuries not only in music but in many other fields as well, and they furnish a vivid social commentary on the times…Perhaps more important, the appearance and continuing publication of these elementary manuals show that the violin had ceased to be the sole property and concern of professional violinists and that it had begun to appeal to a far broader social group among players.[28]

Towards the end of the seventeenth century and the beginning of the eighteenth century, numerous self-instruction books were published for stringed instruments, particularly the violin. These violin tutors were designed for amateurs, not professional violinists. Between 1658 and 1731, over thirty amateur violin instruction books were published.[29] A sampling of these early publications include John Lenton's *The Gentleman's Diversion* (1693); John Playford's *A Brief Introduction to the Skill of Musick* (the 1658 second edition contained a section entitled "Playing on the Treble Violin"); *Nolens Volens* or *You shall learn to Play on the Violin whether you will or no* (1695, author anonymous); *The Self-Instructor on the Violin* (1695, author anonymous); Peter Prelleur's *The Modern Musick-Master* (1731); and Robert Crome's *The Fiddle New Model'd* (1741) for violin, and his cello tutor *The compleat tutor for the violoncello* (c.1763-1776). Notable features of tutors written by composers such as Crome and Prelleur, were illustrations of the violin fingerboard to assist beginning violinists in knowing where to place their fingers (Crome also included a cello fingerboard illustration in his violoncello tutor). Music historian Robin Stowell asserted that these early violin tutors enhanced the status of playing the violin: "These publications served a valuable purpose in helping the violin rapidly to gain social respectability in competition with the viol."[30]

SECTION 1.14

PIECE: MINUET

The five minuets in this string sampler (the same minuet, arranged in five keys) come from Robert Crome's 1741 violin tutor: *The Fiddle New Model'd, or a Useful Introduction for the Violin, Exemplify'd with familiar Dialogues*. Crome explained why he felt the need to write his violin method book:

The Fiddle is a difficult Instrument to learn because there are no fix'd Places to stop the Fingers on; for when a scholar is taught to play in one Key, beginning in another Key alters the situation of the Fingers so much that we in a manner undo all we were doing before…I have drawn a Scale for every practical Key, by representing the Finger Board of the Fiddle with strings and placing Spots thereon, to show where the Fingers should be put to stop each Note in tune, and though the scholar can't at first stop with Exactness, he will see where the Fingers should be put. Though I am satisfy'd these Scales will be of great use for stopping in Tune, nevertheless we must depend on the Ear as Umpire."[31]

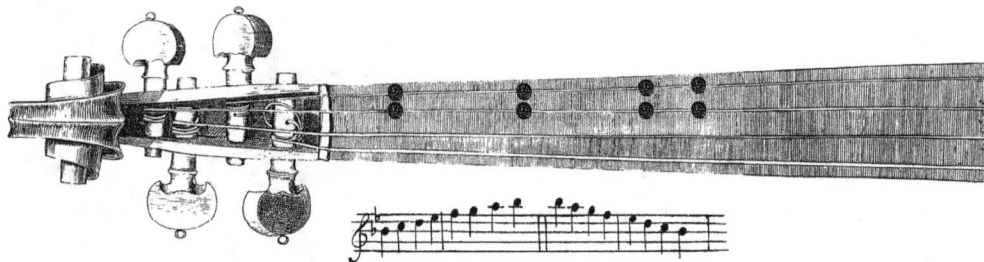

Fig. 1.6 *Crome fingerboard and scale*

Crome's tutor, designed for beginning amateur violinists, provided instruction and musical examples, including illustrations of the violin fingerboard showing the appropriate finger placement for specific keys. Crome also included a minuet, transposed in eight keys, to illustrate the appropriate fingering pattern to use. A sample image of Crome's violin fingerboard illustration is provided in figure 1.6, and his *Minuet in the key of C* is shown in figure 1.7. It is interesting to note that Crome used this same *Minuet* as the first piece in a tutor he wrote for the violoncello entitled *The compleat tutor for the violoncello, containing the best & easiest instructions for learners.*[32]

Fig. 1.7 *Crome Minuet, key of C*

TECHNIQUE TIPS: Use Crome's fingerboard illustration and the photos provided in the sheet music to determine where to place your fingers for each finger pattern. The finger patterns used in the featured *Minuets* are the standard finger patterns you'll need to play any music in any key.

STUDY UNIT 2—BAROQUE MUSIC

BAROQUE MUSIC SECTIONS

Fig. 2.1 *Venetian musician, 1723*

SECTION 2.1

BAROQUE MUSICAL PERIOD OVERVIEW (1600-1750)

1)   **Ornate Baroque art, architecture and music.** The term Baroque was derived from the Portuguese word *barocco* which means an "irregularly shaped pearl." There were negative associations first associated with the use of the term Baroque, and when applied to art and architecture, it implied something that was unbalanced, overly ornate and extravagant. These negative associations have disappeared, and in music, Baroque now describes a style that sounds grandiose, expansive, and is often ornamented and filled with energy and movement.

2)   **Scientific discoveries and experimentation.** The Baroque era was a time of scientific investigation and discovery, and significant scientific advances were made by prominent individuals such as Sir Isaac Newton who formulated the theory of gravity; Johannes Kepler, and Galileo Galilei, who expanded on Copernicus's theories of the movement of planets; Sir William Harvey, who defined the circulation of blood; and René Descartes who made advances in the field of mathematics. Experimentation also took place in music, and composers experimented with new sounds, effects, compositional styles and instrumental techniques.

3) **Absolute monarchy and the rising middle class.** This period is sometimes referred to as the Age of Absolutism, a time when the concept of the divine right of kings resulted in absolute rule by "God-chosen" monarchs. European kings such as Louis XIV of France (1638-1715) ruled with the self-described mandate, "I am the state," and his lavish lifestyle is exemplified by his opulent summer palace at Versailles. Members of the middle class were not included in the musical events regularly held by the aristocracy, and the middle class held their own musical events in their homes or in organizations such as *collegium musicums*, groups of citizens who met to play and sing music for their own pleasure.

4) **Religion and war.** Strong religious views were expressed during this era, and two of Europe's main religions were Protestantism and Catholicism. The Protestant Reformation led to the Catholic Church's Counter-Reformation, and many violent religious wars resulted from their differences. Although the Church continued to patronize the arts, its influence was not as great as in past eras, and the aristocracy, merchant class and financiers began to play a more prominent role in supporting the arts. Religion also played a role in the establishment of the American colonies. During the seventeenth century, many Protestant refugees left northern Europe and sought religious freedom in America, and they brought their music traditions with them.

SECTION 2.2

BAROQUE MUSICAL STYLE CHARACTERISTICS

Performing Medium. Vocal and instrumental music were both prominent during this era, and ensembles such as chamber orchestras became popular (the term chamber orchestra was used to describe a small number of instrumentalists who could fit in a room or small hall). Strings were the main section of the chamber orchestra, and woodwinds and brass were used for solo effects. Other performance groups included solo instruments with chamber orchestra (concerto grosso); soloist and orchestra; chorus and chamber orchestra; organ, and harpsichord.

Rhythm. Energetic, driving rhythms were frequently used during the Baroque period. Short, melodic and rhythmic phrases were commonplace, including the basso ostinato, a melody set over a repeated bass pattern. Meters such as 2, 3, 4 and 6 were typical, tempos were faster and slower than earlier periods, and the tempo would often slow towards the end of a piece.

Melody. Major and minor melodies were used, and emotion was frequently expressed through melodic devices such as dissonant intervals. Melodic range during the Baroque era expanded from earlier periods, and techniques such as sequence and imitation were used in constructing melodies. Ornamentation was frequently used, including improvisation. Expressive tools such as dynamics were generally either loud or soft, and gradual increases in dynamics were seldom found.

Harmony. Major and minor scales were generally used as the basis for the tonal centers of pieces. Cadences at the end of sections were strong, and harmonic movement often included modulations and harmonic sequences (repetition of a series of chords at a higher or lower pitch).

Texture. Baroque texture was often polyphonic (a form of musical texture with several interdependent, overlapping melodic lines), with multiple melodies and countermelodies, a continuous bass line, and occasional homophony (musical texture with a melody and chordal accompaniment).

Form. Detailed forms included two and three-part forms, and large forms included: sonata, suite, concerto, concerto grosso, oratorio, cantata, opera and fugue.

SECTION 2.3

PIECE: RONDEAU

Henry Purcell (1659-1695) was an English composer, and although he primarily worked as a musician and composer for the English royal court, during the last five years of his life, he also wrote theater music for over 40 plays. During this period, theater music was often called incidental music because it was written to supplement a spoken drama and was not part of the actual play. *Rondeau* was one of the pieces Purcell composed for a play written by a prominent woman playwright, Aphra Behn, and the play was entitled *Abdelazar* or *The Moor's Revenge*. Purcell composed this incidental music in 1695, and scored the music for a string orchestra and harpsichord.[1] There are two aspects to *Rondeau*'s musical form:

1) Purcell's title for this movement implies it is in the musical form of a *rondeau*, a French musical term used during this period to describe a musical composition with a main section or theme which alternates with subsidiary sections or themes (during the Classical music period, the *rondeau* was expanded to become the musical form Rondo).[2]

2) Another aspect of Purcell's *Rondeau*, is that it has the feel of a lively hornpipe dance, a dance similar to the jig, but with a different meter. The country dance version of the hornpipe generally had a 3/2 meter (other versions of the hornpipe used 2/4 and 4/4 meters). Meter is a term which describes how the beats in each measure are grouped in stressed and unstressed patterns, and a 3/2 meter typically means three half notes are grouped in each measure with a stress on the first beat as follows: ONE-two-three. Purcell's *Rondeau* has a 3/2 meter, and the rhythmic lively pulse of the music clearly provides it with the feel of a hornpipe dance. During the 16th-18th centuries, composers often used the spirited country dance rhythm of the hornpipe dance for movements in dance suites and incidental theater music.[3]

If *Rondeau's* melody sounds familiar, it could be because Purcell's *Rondeau* theme was later used by Benjamin Britten in 1945 as the basis of Britten's piece *The Young Person's Guide to the Orchestra,* "Variations and Fugue on a Theme of Purcell."

TECHNIQUE TIPS: This piece is in a *rondeau* form, and this arrangement of Purcell's *Rondeau* has the following musical structure: **A B C A** (the main theme is represented by the letter A, and the other letters represent contrasting themes). As you play this music, listen to see if you can tell the difference between the following sections of Purcell's *Rondeau*: section A measures 1-8; section B measures 9-16; section C measures 17-24; and section A returns in measure 25 to the end. The tempo or speed of the music should have the sprightly feel of a hornpipe dance, and you should be able to feel the strong three beat pulse in every measure.

SECTION 2.4

PIECE: "HORNPIPE" FROM WATER MUSIC

George Friederich Handel (1685-1759) was the composer of "Hornpipe," one of the pieces from his *Water Music* suite. Although Handel was born in Germany, he spent most of his adult life as a musician in England. He showed an early interest in music, but his father, a barber-surgeon, wanted him to be a lawyer. Handel's musical talent was so apparent that his father finally gave his reluctant approval for him to study music. Following Handel's graduation from the University of Halle, he became a church organist for a brief period, and then moved to Hamburg where he composed his first opera in 1705. In 1706, Handel moved to Italy for several years to further his interest in Italian music, and while there, he received acclaim as a promising young composer.

In 1709, Handel was offered the position of Music Director for the Elector of Hanover, and he returned to Germany. Handel felt stifled as a composer there, and remained in Germany for only a brief time. He requested extended leaves of absence from his music position so he could travel to London to compose and produce operas and other musical works. In 1714, Handel was still in England and was faced with a dilemma when his German employer, the Elector of Hanover, was appointed George I of England. Handel apparently was able to redeem himself with the king, and was offered a position as a court composer for the king. Handel spent most of his musical life in London, supported by the patronage of the royal family and other prominent members of the aristocracy. He also sought ways to make money through other means such as through the sale of subscription tickets (tickets were pre-sold to a series of concerts), and by seeking commissions for his music. Handel was internationally recognized as a superb composer of music in almost all genres: instrumental works, operas, oratorios, sacred vocal music, and keyboard music, and his compositional techniques foreshadowed many progressive elements of the Romantic era.[4]

Fig. 2.2 *The Thames and the City, 1746-47*

Handel wrote his orchestral suite, *Water Music,* in 1717 to provide musical entertainment for King George I and his guests as they traveled along the Thames River in a royal barge procession (the orchestra of 50 musicians was on its own barge). The musical definition of a suite is a collection of pieces, put together in an ordered manner. During the Baroque era, pieces in a suite were often in dance forms such as: *prelude, allemande, courante, saraband, gigue, bourre, gavotte,* and *minuet.* After the Baroque era, suites often were pieces extracted from a larger work such as *The Nutcracker Suite.*

TECHNIQUE TIPS: This piece, "Hornpipe" from Handel's *Water Music,* has the 3/2 meter and musical form of the country dance version of the hornpipe. Handel indicated that this movement should be played *allegro* (a quick, lively and fast tempo), and that it should begin with the dynamic level of *f* (meaning *forte,* or play loudly with a strong sound). Be sure to contrast the dynamics of the beginning section (measures 1-11), with the **mp** section beginning in measure 12 (**mp** means *mezzo piano,* or moderately soft). The main theme and *forte* section return in measure 28 to the end.

SECTION 2.5

PIECE: LA FOLIA MEDLEY

This arrangement of *La Folia* is a medley of *La Folia* music composed by Marin Marais, Arcangelo Corelli, and Antonio Vivaldi. Marin Marais (1656-1728) was a French composer and studied composition with the prominent French composer Jean-Baptiste Lully (1632-1687). Marais was a viol virtuoso, and became a member of the King Louis XIV's royal orchestra, eventually acquiring the honored position of *Ordinaire de la chambre du Roi pour la viole* (roughly translated to mean "regular violist of the King's chambers"). Marais composed instrumental music and operas, and is particularly noted for his viol compositions. He published five collections of viol music, comprising more than 550 pieces. The name of his arrangement of *La Folia* was "Couplets des Folies d'Espagne," and it came from his Book 2 collection of viol music, *Pièces de viole,* published in 1701.[5]

Arcangelo Corelli (1653-1713) was an Italian composer and violinist, and was particularly famous for his solo sonata, trio sonata and concerto instrumental compositions. Some of his patrons included Queen Christina of Sweden, Cardinal Benedetto Pamphili and Cardinal Pietro Ottoboni. Corelli's version of "La Follia" came from his *Sonata No. 12, Op. 5*, a set of 12 sonatas published in 1700, and he dedicated *Op.5* to the Electress Sophie Charlotte of Brandenburg. *Op. 5* was one of Corelli's most popular collections of music, and at least 42 editions of *Op. 5* were published by 1800 (advances in music publishing during this time period contributed to the widespread popularity and accessibility of Corelli's music).[6]

Corelli's *Op. 5* was a set of 12 sonatas for solo violin with a *basso continuo* accompaniment. The term *basso continuo* (also known as continuo or figured bass) describes a bass part in a composition, generally annotated with numbers to indicate harmonic intervals that should be played above the bass line. During the Baroque period, the continuo was generally performed by a keyboard player (such as a harpsichord) to provide a harmonic accompaniment, and a cello frequently played the continuo part along with the harpsichord.

Op. 5 is a set of sonatas, and the word sonata comes from the Italian word *suonare* meaning "to sound" or "to be played," as opposed to *cantata*, a vocal work which means "to be sung." A sonata is an instrumental form of music and describes a multi-movement work for an instrument, often with accompaniment. The term has had varied meanings during different music eras, and during the early Baroque period, sonata was an imprecise designation for an independent piece of music with several movements, for a few instruments with a basso continuo accompaniment. The trio sonata was one of the most popular forms of sonatas used during the Baroque period, and the instrumentation generally used in trio sonatas consisted of two violins and continuo.

Corelli was a central figure in the evolution of the sonata. Two types of sonatas were popular during the Baroque era: church sonatas (*sonate da chiesa*) and chamber sonatas (*sonate da camera*). Corelli's church sonatas, or *sonate da chiesa*, generally had a four movement structure of slow-fast-slow-fast. The first movement was often a processional, French-overture type of movement; the second movement was generally fast and imitative, often a fugue; the third movement was in a lyrical, aria style; and the fourth movement often was a fast, bipartite dance form. Corelli's chamber sonatas, or *sonate da camera*, were basically a collection of binary dances based on French dances with no set number of movements. These two forms of sonatas, church and chamber sonatas, eventually merged before the Baroque period ended. During the Classical period, sonata came to mean a multi-movement work for a solo instrument with piano accompaniment, or piano alone.[7] [8]

Antonio Vivaldi (1678-1741) was a virtuoso violinist and composer of instrumental music, operas and sacred music. He was born in Venice, Italy, and studied the violin with his father, Giovanni Battista, a professional violinist. At the age of twenty-six, Vivaldi was appointed *maestro di violino* at the *Pio Ospedale della Pieta*, one of four Venetian institutions for illegitimate, orphaned, or abandoned girls. This particular orphanage specialized in music and had many fine musicians and an exceptional orchestra. Vivaldi's responsibilities eventually included teacher of violin, director of concerts, choirmaster, and composer. Many of his symphonies and concertos were composed for student and faculty associates of la Pieta.

Vivaldi earned a living as a musician not only through his affiliation with la Pieta, but also through the sale of his music in manuscript and published forms. He composed over 800 works such as approximately 500 instrumental concertos, over 90 solo and trio sonatas, and a vast array of instrumental chamber music, operas, masses, oratorios and cantatas. Vivaldi's "Variations on La Follia" is part of a set of 12 trio sonatas, *Op. 1, No. 12* (the earliest known edition is dated 1705). *Op. 1, No. 12* was scored for two violins and a basso continuo part.[9]

La folia originated as a dance song in the late 15th century in countries such as Portugal. The word *folia* means "mad" or "empty-headed," and apparently was used because the dance originally was so fast and tumultuous, that it appeared as if the dancers were crazy or mad. Later versions of *la folia* adopted a more stately and moderately paced tempo, and *la folia* soon became popular in other countries such as Spain, Italy, France and England. Many composers have written *folia* variations, and just a few of the noted musicians who have done so include: Marais, Corelli, Vivaldi, Lully, Scarlatti, J.S. Bach, C.P.E. Bach, Grieg, Liszt and Rachmaninoff.

This version of *La Folia* is a set of variations movements, often called variation sets. The main theme is clearly expressed in the first eight measures of the piece, followed by increasingly complex rhythmic and melodic variations (the harmonic structure remains the same). This piece also uses an *ostinato*, a term which means "obstinate" in Italian. An *ostinato* is a short musical pattern, *e.g.* a melodic, rhythmic or harmonic figure, persistently repeated throughout a composition. The theme of this piece may be described as an *ostinato*, and as mentioned earlier, the *La folia* theme or *ostinato* is used as the subject of a series of melodic-rhythmic variation movements.[10] [11]

TECHNIQUE TIPS: This arrangement of *La Folia* includes four variations of the *La folia* theme, and features the compositions of Marais, Corelli and Vivaldi. Use a moderately slow and stately tempo as you begin the piece. The main theme is simply stated in the first eight measures, and is then repeated, ending with a slight variation in the harmony. The different variations of the theme in this arrangement will require the use of varied bowing techniques such as slightly separated notes for Corelli's Variation 2 (beginning in measure 33); slurred triplets for Vivaldi's Variation 3 (beginning in measure 41); and short, fast 16th notes for Corelli's Variation 4 (this variation begins in measure 57, and you may want to play this section using the upper 1/3 of your bow). If some of these variations are too difficult for you, try playing the main theme found in the first eight measures of the piece along with the piano accompaniment or recording during the technically challenging variations. If you're playing this piece with the piano accompaniment or a recorded version of this arrangement, note how Vivaldi's Variation 3 has a descant part, playing a third above the melody (Vivaldi's original *La Follia* score was written for 2 violins with an accompaniment).

SECTION 2.6

PIECE: DOUBLE VIOLIN CONCERTO IN A MINOR, 1ST MOVEMENT

Fig. 2.3 *Antonio Vivaldi*

Antonio Vivaldi (1678-1741) composed his violin concerto for two violins, *Op. 3 No. 8* in 1711. Vivaldi wrote an estimated 500 instrumental concertos, and approximately 40 of them were double concertos (for two solo instruments). Vivaldi was particularly renowned for his contributions to the development of the concerto form. A concerto is an instrumental composition for solo instrument(s), and is often structured in three movements with the sequence fast-slow-fast. The accompaniment for a concerto typically is an orchestra. Prior to Vivaldi, many elements of the concerto were not standardized. Vivaldi helped establish the three movement form of the concerto, as well as inner features of the movements.[12]

Vivaldi dedicated his *Op. 3* to the Grand Prince Ferdinando of Tuscany. Dedications often were a way to try to gain the favor (and financial support) of prominent patrons. Although Vivaldi sold much of his music through commissioned manuscripts, he also gained some profit from the printed sales of his compositions. *Op. 3* was published by Estienne Roger, an Amsterdam publisher who apparently revolutionized European music publishing during the eighteenth century. Roger favored the engraved method of printing, a process which was more pleasing to the eye, more flexible, and better suited for short runs than the movable system of printing being used by most publishers in Italy during this time. Roger's commercial success was not only due to the new technology he used, but also was the result of increased consumer demand and the wide network of selling agents he had developed throughout Europe. Amateur musicians were apparently eager to acquire new sheet music they could play, and scholar Michael Talbot described how this contributed to composers from Italy commencing a "flight to Amsterdam" to have their works published by Roger so they could profit from the sale of their music:

> Italian composers purportedly began to write music with the partly amateur northern European market in mind. The result was an increased sensitivity to fashion, a certain cosmopolitanism, a restraint in matters of instrumental technique and an avoidance of those elements of *bizzarria* (deliberate strangeness) which might captivate an Italian connoisseur but would be found freakish and unnatural by a Dutch or English gentleman."[13]

Op. 3 was titled "L'estro armonico" which means "The Musical Inspiration" or "The Harmonious Fancy." It is a collection of 12 concertos for solo violin or groups of violins with a small orchestra. "L'Estro armonico" had a tremendous impact on composers in Northern Europe. After this work was published, several composers traveled to Italy to take lessons with Vivaldi, while others paid him the more subtle compliment of making arrangements of his music (such as J.S. Bach, who arranged five of Vivaldi's concertos from "L'Estro armonico" for keyboard).

TECHNIQUE TIPS: The first movement from Vivaldi's *Op. 3, No. 8* is used in this arrangement. Although it is a double concerto, in this arrangement, the melody features the primary parts of both solo instruments. The tempo is *allegro*, meaning use a quick, lively and fast tempo. You also may want to try using a short bow stroke in the upper third of your bow for the fast passages. Music scholar David Boyden described how Baroque string players often used a separated, slightly articulated bow stroke for fast passages:

> In musical terms the bow stroke of the early eighteenth century produced what was, by modern standards, a relatively light, clearly articulated tone; and the normal nuanced style of the full bow stroke was far more expressive than the modern counterpart. A kind of non-legato stroke must have resulted from the rapid wrist articulation of fast notes, approaching the modern *spiccato* in effect, but attained without actually leaving the string.[14]

SECTION 2.7

PIECE: "PRELUDE" FROM CELLO SUITE NO. 1

Fig. 2.4 *J. S. Bach*

Johann Sebastian Bach (1685-1750) wrote his *Cello Suite No. 1* in 1620. Bach's career as a composer and musician included positions such as church organist in the towns of Arnstadt and Mühlhausen; court organist and concertmaster for the Duke of Weimar; director of music for Prince Leopold of Anhalt at Cöthen; cantor of St. Thomas Church; and civic director of music for Leipzig. Bach's Leipzig position was one of the most prestigious musical positions in Germany at the time, and included responsibilities such as: music for the four main churches in Leipzig, musical training of students at a boarding school associated with St. Thomas, and various duties for the city of Leipzig 's musical affairs. In 1729, Bach added to his Leipzig responsibilities when he assumed leadership of the Leipzig *collegium musicum*, a voluntary organization founded by Telemann in 1704. Members of this *collegium musicum* included university students and professional musicians, and they contributed to the musical culture of the community with weekly concerts.

Bach was the father of twenty children: seven with his first wife, his cousin Maria Barbara Bach, and thirteen with his second wife, Anna Magdalena (half of his children did not survive past childhood). Bach taught his children music, and his family often performed together as a vocal and instrumental concert group. Some of Bach's children went on to become noted musicians such as Carl Philipp Emanuel Bach and Johann Christian Bach.

Bach's musical output was related to his employment, thus while he was employed as an organist at Arnstadt, Mühlhausen and Wiemer, he composed a large number of organ works. During his tenure as Kapellmeister at Cöthen, he wrote large amounts of instrumental works, and while he was Cantor at Leipzig, he wrote hundreds of cantatas and other sacred vocal works for church services. During Bach's term as leader of Leipzig 's *collegium musicum*, he wrote new instrumental music and he also created new arrangements of instrumental works he had written in Cöthen. It is interesting to note that Bach regarded the purpose of all of his music as being "to the glory of God," and he often inscribed his compositions with letters such as S.D.G. (the initials stood for *soli Deo Gloria*, meaning, "to God alone be glory").[15]

Bach composed his *Six Suites for Solo Cello* in 1620 while he was residing in Cöthen under the patronage of Prince Leopold. Bach's cello suites were not typical for this time period. Prior to the mid-18th century, solo music for cello was not only uncommon, but Baroque music for cellists rarely called for technically demanding skills found in Bach's cello suites such as multiple stops, complex bowing, *barriolage,* arpeggios, and left hand virtuosity.[16]

TECHNIQUE TIPS: Bach's unaccompanied *Cello Suite No. 1* is in the musical form of a suite. A suite may be described as a collection of pieces, put together in an ordered manner. During the Baroque era, pieces in a suite were often in dance forms such as: allemande, courante, saraband, gigue, bourre, gavotte, and minuet. The excerpt used in this arrangement is the "Prelude" from Bach's *Cello Suite No. 1*. Bach often began his suites and sonatas with a prelude, a piece with an improvisatory style which serves as a prelude or introduction to other pieces in the musical composition. This piece calls for numerous string crossings and ends with a triple stop. To play the triple stop, play the bottom two notes as a chord first, then the top two notes as a chord (for a brief moment, the middle note will be played by itself as a string crossing as your pivot between the two chords).

SECTION 2.8

PIECE: "ALLEGRO" FROM BRANDENBURG CONCERTO NO. 5

There are six concertos in the Brandenburg collection, and Bach composed this music over a period of several years. At the time Bach compiled these concertos into the set known as the *Brandenburg Concertos*, he was the court music director for Prince Leopold of Cöthen. The court orchestra at Cöthen was reknowned for its large size and fine players, and it is likely that Bach wrote this music for Cöthen orchestra performances (some music scholars suggest that some of the concertos were written even earlier, while Bach worked for the Duke of Weimar). When Bach traveled to Berlin to make final arrangements for a new harpsichord he was acquiring for Prince Leopold, he was asked to play for the Margrave Christian Ludwig of Brandenburg. The Margrave was apparently so pleased with Bach's performance, that he requested music for his library. In response, Bach dedicated his Brandenburg Concertos to the Margrave of Brandenburg, and in 1721, sent a dedicatory letter to the Margrave along with a manuscript copy of the music.[17] The following excerpt from Bach's dedicatory letter illustrates the effusive praise and somewhat obsequious language musicians often used to curry favor with potential patrons:

> I had a few years ago the pleasure of playing before Your Royal Highness, at your Highness's command, and whereas I noted on that occasion that the modest talent for music that Heaven has bestowed upon me found favor in Your eyes, and whereas in departing your Royal Highness deigned to honor me with the charge to send Your Highness some compositions of mine, therefore I have, in accordance with Your Highness's most gracious charge, taken the liberty of fulfilling my most humble duty to Your Royal Highness with the present concertos, which I have scored for several instruments.[18]

TECHNIQUE TIPS: This musical arrangement is taken from the first movement of Bach's *Brandenburg Concerto No. 5*. It is in the musical form of a *concerto grosso*. A *concerto grosso* is an instrumental concerto for a small group of soloists called the *concertino*, which play in contrast to the main body of instrumentalists or orchestra called the *ripieno* or *tutti*. Bach scored *Concerto No. 5* for three solo instruments: flute, violin and harpsichord (it was designed to feature the new harpsichord Bach brought back from Berlin). These solo instruments (the *concertino*), play their part in contrast with the orchestra (or *tutti*). This melody of this arrangement features both the *concertino* and *tutti* parts, otherwise, there would be frequent rests. This movement is marked *allegro*, a lively and brisk tempo. As you play the rapid sixteenth notes, use short bows in the upper third of your bow.

SECTION 2.9

PIECE: "KYRIE" FROM MESSA A 4 CON VIOLINI

Maurizio Cazzati (1616-1678) was an Italian composer who wrote sacred and secular music. He was *maestro di cappella* of churches and courts such as S Andrea, Mantua; the court of Scipione Gonzaga, Prince of Bozzolo; the Accademia della Morte at Ferrara; S Maria Maggiore, Bergamo; S Petronio, Bologna; the court of the Duchess Anna Isabella Gonzaga at Mantua, and the Mantua Cathedral. Cazatti published 66 volumes of music during his lifetime, and although most of his works were sacred, he was noted for his contributions to instrumental music.[19]

Some scholars have asserted that the violin played an important role in the resurgence of the mass in the 17th century, and composers such as Cazatti helped this occur. As described earlier in the Medieval musical period study unit, as a musical form, a mass is a sacred vocal form of music used as part of the worship services for the Catholic Church. During the 17th century, the prominent use of violins in masses primarily took place in *messa concertata,* masses composed for festive ceremonial occasions. Music scholar Anne Schnoebelen described the violin's contribution to the revitalization of the mass:

> The violin was the favoured instrument of the ceremonial mass by the 1630s. Its role changed from providing extra-liturgical canzonas and sonatas to being incorporated into the fabric and form of the mass…The addition of violins was a turning point in the development of the mass, revitalizing it into a form that would attract composers for the next 250 years.[20]

TECHNIQUE TIPS: The excerpt chosen for this piece is taken from Cazzati's "Kyrie," one of the sections in his *Messa a 4 con violini, e ripieni a beneplacito, Opera XIV,* published in 1653. This music may be categorized as a *messa concertata*, a festive ceremonial mass used for special occasions such as liturgical feasts. As the title of the selected piece indicates, four violins were specifically called for to perform this work. This excerpt includes three instrumental ritornello sections which were used by Cazzati to contrast with the vocal sections of the "Kyrie." At times, Cazzati's "Kyrie" instrumental music uses and reworks motives from the vocal music in preceding sections; at other times, he introduces new thematic material. Cazzati's instrumental music sections sound as if they were independent and spirited dance pieces, and you may want to try using sprightly, lively bowing to play this arrangement of Cazzati's "Kyrie."

SECTION 2.10

PIECE: MESSIAH MEDLEY

Fig. 2.5 *Handel*

George Friederich Handel (1685-1759) composed *Messiah,* an oratorio, in 1741. An oratorio is a large musical work, and is often based on a sacred text or religious topic, with soloists, chorus and orchestra. Although many musical elements in an oratorio are similar to those used in an opera, oratorios are generally performed as a concert, and since no costumes, sets or acting are used, they are less costly to produce than an opera. One of the additional benefits of performing an oratorio in countries such as England during the Baroque period, was that they could be performed during the Lenten season (operas were prohibited from being performed during Lent, a time of fasting and penitence customarily 40 days preceding Easter). Although the subject matter of Baroque oratorios often was religious, Handel's oratorios were not composed for religious services. Instead, they were performed in public theaters to entertain a paying audience. Today, oratorios such as *Messiah* are performed in churches as well as in concert halls.[21]

Most of Handel's oratorios were based on stories from the Old Testament. *Messiah* is an exception; it is Handel's only English oratorio that uses the Old Testament and New Testament, and is centered around the life and mission of the Messiah, Jesus Christ. The libretto (text) was compiled by Charles Jennens, and Jennens primarily used scriptures from the King James Bible as the text. Handel composed the music for *Messiah* in 24 days, and the oratorio is about 2 ½ hours long. *Messiah* was first performed in Dublin, Ireland in 1742, and its London premier was during the Lenten season in 1743. Handel's *Messiah* uses the standard Baroque oratorio small forms of arias, duets, recitatives and choruses. It is divided into three parts: part I prophecies the Messiah's birth and man's redemption through him; Part II describes Christ's redeeming sacrifice; and in Part III, the promise of eternal life through the redemption of Christ is celebrated.[22] [23]

TECHNIQUE TIPS: This medley is comprised of excerpts from two pieces from Handel's *Messiah*: "He Shall Feed His Flock Like a Shepherd," and an excerpt from "Hallelujah Chorus," the last piece in Part II of *Messiah*. "He Shall Feed His Flock Like a Shepherd" is in the musical form of an air, meaning a song. Use smooth, flowing bows for this slow, lyrical air. Handel's musical directions for this piece are *larghetto e piano*, meaning play softly and use a broad, large and stately tempo and style. The tempo of the second excerpt, Handel's "Hallelujah Chorus," is *allegro*, indicating a fast tempo should be used. Handel's "Hallelujah Chorus" should be played in a joyful, vigorous manner to capture the rejoicing nature of the text.

He Shall Feed His Flock Like a Shepherd (*text, second verse*)

Come unto him, all ye that labour,
Come unto him, that are heavy laden,
And he will give you rest,

Take his yoke upon you, and learn of him;
For he is meek and lowly of heart;
and ye shall find rest,
and ye shall find rest unto your souls.

Hallelujah Chorus (*text, excerpt*)

Hallelujah! Hallelujah!
Hallelujah! Hallelujah! Hallelujah!

Hallelujah! Hallelujah!
Hallelujah! Hallelujah! Hallelujah!

For the Lord God Omnipotent reigneth.
Hallelujah! Hallelujah!
Hallelujah! Hallelujah!

For the Lord God Omnipotent reigneth.
Hallelujah! Hallelujah!
Hallelujah! Hallelujah!

And He shall reign for ever and ever.
King of Kings, and Lord of Lords,
King of Kings, and Lord of Lords,

And he shall reign for ever and ever,
King of Kings, and Lord of Lords.
King of Kings, and Lord of Lords.
and He shall reign for ever and ever.

King of Kings, and Lord of Lords.
Hallelujah! Hallelujah! Hallelujah!
Hallelujah! Hallelujah!

SECTION 2.11

PIECE: "ARIOSO" FROM CANTATA NO. 156

Bach composed his *Cantata No. 156* in 1729, and "Arioso" is the first movement found in this cantata. The term cantata means "to be sung," and the musical form of a cantata may be described as a sacred or secular vocal work with instrumental accompaniment. Cantatas are often divided into sections such as choruses, solos, recitatives and arias. During the Baroque era, Bach was a prolific composer of cantatas, and he composed many of them for church services (approximately 200 of his church cantatas are extant). Bach's first movement of *Cantata No. 156* is an instrumental *sinfonia*, a form which Bach often used as a single-movement instrumental prelude or introductory movement to other pieces in a musical work *(sinfonia* later came to mean a light version of a symphony). The songlike character of this first movement has contributed to instrumental transcriptions of this movement often being titled "arioso," a term which means "like an aria" or melodious.[24]

During the Baroque period, it was a common practice for musicians to reuse and rework some of their melodies in other pieces (Handel and Vivaldi were particularly well-known for this practice). Some scholars have proposed that Bach first used "Arioso's" melody in a now lost D minor oboe concerto. After using a version of the same melody in his *Cantata No. 156*, Bach apparently reused the melody for the second movement of his harpsichord *Sonata in F minor*. Even more interesting, some scholars have found similarities between Bach's "Arioso" melody and a piece written by another prominent German musician, Georg Philipp Telemann. These scholars have speculated that Bach modeled his melody after the first movement of Telemann's *G-major concerto for solo oboe or flute and strings* (TWV 51:G2). They described this process as: Bach used "transformative imitation to turn preexistent music by another composer into a distinctive expression of his own compositional voice."[25]

TECHNIQUE TIPS: The title of this cantata is *Ich steh mit einem Fuss im Grabe*, tranlated to mean "I stand with one foot in the grave." "Arioso," the first movement in this cantata serves as a lyrical and peaceful instrumental introduction to the rest of the cantata. The tempo is marked *adagio*, meaning use a slow, leisurely tempo. As you play the flowing lines of the melody, use slurs and smooth bow changes when needed.

STUDY UNIT 3—CLASSICAL MUSIC

CLASSICAL MUSIC SECTIONS

Fig. 3.1 *Mozart with his father and sister*

SECTION 3.1

CLASSICAL MUSICAL PERIOD OVERVIEW (1750-1825)

1) **The Age of Enlightenment.** This period, also called the Age of Reason, was a time when the philosophies and classical traditions of ancient Greece and Rome were idealized, and reason, logic and restraint were emulated. In music, this led to forms which stressed clarity, balance, restraint and the logical expression of clear musical ideas.

2) **The Industrial Revolution.** During the late eighteenth and early nineteenth century, the Industrial Revolution caused abrupt change in the social and economic order as men and women, formerly accustomed to agricultural pursuits, moved to cities to work in factories and other forms of large-scale industrial production. In cities such as London, class distinctions divided the wealthy upper-class from members of the lower-class, and this later led to philanthropic efforts by the upper-class to educate and improve the lives of lower-class factory workers through free public concerts and inexpensive or free classes (including sight-singing classes and violin classes for adults).

3) **Public concerts.** The Enlightenment promoted the concept that all human life should be enriched by the arts, and that culture should not be the exclusive provenance of the aristocracy. Public concerts, which had first begun in the mid-1600s in places such as taverns and meeting halls, provided entertainment by local music societies (also known as academies or *collegium musicums*), with members who were primarily amateur musicians. This form of entertainment

flourished during the Classical period, and some of these groups evolved into professional orchestras such as the Leipzig Gewandhaus Orchestra.

Public concerts were also offered in forms such as subscription concerts, where the paying general public had the opportunity to hear some of the same professional musicians and orchestral concerts formerly offered only to the aristocracy. The concept behind subscription concerts, was to sell prepaid tickets to a series of concerts, thus guaranteeing a financial return to the composer, musicians and promoters. Although the patronage system still was an important source of financial support for musicians during this era, composers began to have a new source of income through subscription concert ticket sales. Mozart wrote many of his orchestral compositions for subscription concerts in Vienna, and Haydn wrote some of his most famous symphonies, the London Symphonies, for a series of subscription concerts (Haydn participated in these subscription concerts after his service to his patrons, the royal Esterhazy family ended). By the end of the late eighteenth century, public concerts were held throughout most major cities in Europe, and at these subscription concerts, the middle class could hear the latest concerto, symphony or traveling virtuoso, for the price of a ticket.

4) **Political change and democracy.** The French Revolution (1789-99) and the American Revolution (1775-83) both espoused the ideals of a republic governed by the people, not the aristocracy. The eventual transfer of power from the monarchy to the middle class led to new rights and freedoms for many, including opportunities to participate in cultural activities previously denied to the general public.

SECTION 3.2

CLASSICAL MUSICAL STYLE CHARACTERISTICS

Performing Medium. Music during this era was commonly performed by ensembles and instruments such as chamber orchestras; symphony orchestras (expanded to include string, woodwind, brass, and percussion sections); orchestra with soloist; chamber ensembles; and large choral groups for forms such as operas and oratorios.

Rhythm. Simple, straightforward rhythms with a strong, steady beat and tempo prevailed.

Melody. Melodies composed during the Classical period frequently employed symmetrical phrases with clearly marked beginnings and endings. Melodies with scalar patterns or melodies that outlined chords were common, and lyrical passages were often ornamented. Relatively few dynamic markings appear in music scores from this era, and when they were present, they often indicated immediate change. For this reason, many music scholars assume that the dynamics of the Classical period were generally changed or "terraced" (immediately loud or soft).

Harmony. Simple harmonic structure prevailed during this era such as use of the primary triads (I, IV, and V, and frequently the dominant seventh). Harmony was mainly diatonic (major and minor harmonies), harmonic progressions were simple, and non-harmonic tones were not used as frequently as they were during the Baroque period.

Texture. The texture of this period was primarily homophonic: a melody with chordal accompaniment. During development sections, polyphony was sometimes used.

Form. Detailed forms frequently used during this period included sonata form, rondo, minuet and trio, and theme and variation. Large forms included genres such as concertos, string quartets, sonatas, symphonies, operas, oratorios and masses.

SECTION 3.3

PIECE: AVE VERUM CORUPUS

Wolfgang Amadeus Mozart (1756-91) composed *Ave Verum Corpus, K. 618* in 1791. Mozart was one of the most influential composers during the Classical period. He wrote over 600 musical works, and excelled in composing all of the major genres of music popular during his era such as opera, orchestral music, chamber and solo instrumental music, songs and sacred vocal music.

Mozart was born in 1756 in Salzburg, and was taught music by his father, Leopold, a violinist and composer. Wolfgang was a musical prodigy, and began composing and performing publicly from the age of six. His father took him on performance tours throughout Europe, and Mozart not only had the opportunity to play before wealthy patrons and nobility in cities such as Paris, London and Munich, but he also was exposed many different forms of music in his travels (these experiences contributed to Mozart's mastery of a wide variety of styles in his compositions).

Mozart did not choose to follow the traditional, patronage system career path taken by most musicians during his era, thus he did not seek an appointment as a composer to a wealthy patron. Although he worked for a number of years for the Archbishop of Salzburg, Mozart felt the patronage system was too restrictive, and he moved to Vienna in 1781 to pursue a musical career on his own. In 1782, he married Constanze Weber, a singer, and they had six children. Mozart was well-received as a musician in Vienna, and he earned a living by teaching, giving concerts, procuring commissions for his music, publishing his music, and later in his career, as a court musician to the Hapsburg court. However, Mozart and his wife were unable to manage finances well, and as a result, they were frequently in debt. Mozart died from rheumatic fever on December 5, 1791.[1]

Ave Verum Corpus is a short, sacred work composed by Mozart in 1791 for the feast of Corpus Christi. Mozart composed this piece six months before his death. The musical form is a motet. A motet is often defined as a vocal piece with a sacred text, musically composed in the style of the period. The musical form of motet has evolved throughout music history. During the 13th-15th centuries, motets were sacred, unaccompanied choral works, often based on a preexisting melody and text. New melodies were then added to the preexisting melody, usually in counterpoint. Beginning in the 16th century, the preexisting melody frequently was secular. Mozart scored his *Ave Verum Corpus* for chorus, strings and continuo.

TECHNIQUE TIPS: Mozart's *Ave Verum Corpus* motet has a homophonic texture (a form of musical texture with a melody and chordal accompaniment), and although the piece is only 45 measures long, the music evokes a simple, yet sublime mood. Mozart indicated the tempo of this piece should be *adagio*, meaning a slow, leisurely tempo should be used. Utilize smooth, flowing bows to play the peaceful and soaring melody of this lovely motet.

SECTION 3.4

PIECE: "ADAGIO" FROM VIOLIN CONCERTO NO. 3

Mozart composed his *Violin Concerto No. 3, K. 216* in 1775, when he was only 19 years old and was residing in Salzburg, Austria. Mozart sometimes referred to this concerto as the Strassburg Concerto, because he used part of a dance tune from the city of Strassburg in the final, third movement of this concerto (the tune was apparently known as the "The Strassburger"). *Violin Concerto No. 3* is an example of Mozart's mastery of the Classical period form of concerto. This concerto is in a three movement structure with the following standard concerto form:

1) A fast first movement in sonata-allegro form (sonata-allegro form consists of an exposition of the theme, development of the theme, and ends with the recapitulation or return of the theme).

2) A slow second movement with an A-B-A theme.

3) A fast third movement in a rondo form.

TECHNIQUE TIPS: This arrangement of Mozart's *Violin Concerto No. 3* is taken from the second, slow movement of the concerto, and is titled "Adagio," indicating a slow, leisurely tempo should be used. This piece features a serene, scalar melody (scalar means to move in the manner of a scale). Noted Mozart scholar Alfred Einstein described this movement as: "an Adagio that seems to have fallen straight from heaven."[2] Use smooth, seamless bows to play the flowing, lyrical melody of this exquisite piece. Bowing techniques and musical elements used to ornament and enhance the beauty of the melody include slurs, triplets, accidentals, trills and dynamic contrast.

SECTION 3.5

PIECE: "ANDANTE" FROM STRING QUARTET NO. 13

Franz Schubert (1797-1828), composed his *String Quartet No. 13 in A minor*, *Op. 29* in 1824. Schubert was an Austrian composer and musician, and was the son of a schoolmaster. Although Schubert died at the young age of thirty-one, he was a prolific composer and wrote symphonies, piano works, chamber music, sacred vocal music and art songs (he composed over 600 art songs called *Lieder*). Although Schubert has been included in this Classical music section for chronological reasons, like Beethoven, Schubert was a composer who bridged the transition between the Classical and Romantic periods. Many music historians regard Schubert as an early Romantic composer due to his use of Romantic compositional techniques such as expanding Classical genres using harmonic color, highly expressive, beautiful melodies and innovative scoring.

When Schubert was young, he was accepted as a choirboy by the Imperial Court Chapel, which included a boarding-school education at the Imperial and Royal City College in Vienna. In addition to his regular studies, Schubert learned the violin and piano, and was a music pupil of the composer Antonio Salieri. Although many of Schubert's peers were required to join the military, Schubert was too short—he was smaller than the minimum height of five feet, thus he avoided the mandatory military conscription for Austrian citizens.

In 1813, Schubert left college, enrolled in a training school for elementary teachers, and in 1814, began teaching at his father's school. Although Schubert would have preferred to have had a full-time career as a composer, financial reasons apparently necessitated that he teach school, and he was only able to compose in his spare time. In 1818, Schubert procured a music teaching position as music master to the children of Count Johann Esterhazy in Hungary. This position gave him more freedom to compose, and by 1819, Schubert's reputation as a composer had increased to the point that he was able to earn a living through his music.

Schubert often met with his friends for domestic evening concerts of his music, gatherings that were called *Schubertiades*. The picture in figure 3.2 illustrates a *Schubertiade* with Schubert playing the piano, the singer Vogl on his right, and his friend von Spaun on his left. Quartet music was performed frequently at these informal *Schubertiade* concerts, and it is interesting to note that in the early 19th century, string quartet music was often composed for and performed by skilled amateurs or professional musicians playing for fun. During the Classical period, string quartets became an extremely popular form of composition. The term string quartet is often defined as a composition using a multi-movement form for four instruments, with the most common instrumentation being two violins, a viola and a cello.[3]

Figure 3.2 *Schubertiade at the home of Josef von Spaun, 1895*

This piece is an arrangement of the second movement from Schubert's *String Quartet No. 13 in Am*, "Andante." Schubert based this movement on a theme he had already composed as incidental music for a play called *Rosamunde, Princess of Cyprus*. This quartet is nicknamed the *Rosamunde Quartet* due to Schubert's recycling of the theme.[4]

TECHNIQUE TIPS: The tempo for this arrangement of Schubert's second movement from his *String Quartet No. 13* is *andante*, meaning play the piece with a moderately slow tempo (*andante* is often considered to be a walking speed). Slurs are used throughout the flowing melody of this piece, and instances where slurs occur with dots over or under the notes indicate a slight separation should be used between the notes (the terms dotted slurs or slurred staccato are often used to describe this technique). Although the dynamics of this piece are predominantly soft (this movement begins with the designation ***mp***, an abbreviation for *mezzo piano* which means moderately soft), dynamic contrast is found in sections with *crescendo* and *decrescendo* markings. *Crescendo* or *cresc.* means to gradually become louder, and is indicated by the sign: ⟨ , and *diminuendo* (*dim.*) or *decrescendo* (*decresc.* or *decr.*), means to gradually become softer, and is indicated by the sign: ⟩ . The piece ends with a fermata sign over the last note: 𝄐 . This sign indicates the note should be held and prolonged at the discretion of the performer or conductor (fermatas are also called a "hold" or the nickname "bird's eye").

SECTION 3.6

PIECE: "ANDANTE" FROM THE EMPEROR QUARTET

(Franz) Joseph Haydn (1732- 1809) composed his *Emperor Quartet, Op. 76, No. 3* in 1797. Haydn (known as Joseph, not Franz to his peers) was an Austrian composer who excelled in virtually all genres of music popular during the Classical period. He was particularly noted for his contributions to the forms of quartets and symphonies. When Haydn was a young boy, he traveled to Vienna to sing as a choirboy at the St. Stephen's Cathedral, and he remained there for the next ten years as he sang in the choir and received a musical education at the choir school. When his voice "broke" (a natural change which occurs in the voice of an adolescent boy), Haydn was no longer able to sing with the boys choir, and the next phase of his life was rather difficult. Haydn described this period in the following words:

> When my voice finally broke, for eight whole years I was forced to eke out a wretched existence by teaching young people. Many geniuses are ruined by this miserable [need to earn their] daily bread, because they lack time to study. This could well have happened to me; I would never have achieved what little I have done, had I not carried on with my zeal for composition during the night. I composed diligently, but not quite correctly, until I finally had the good fortune to learn the true fundamentals of composition from the famous Porpora (who was in Vienna at the time). Finally, owing to a recommendation from the late [Baron] von Fürnberg (who was especially generous to me), I was appointed as director with Count Morzin, and from there as Kapellmeister with his highness Prince [Esterházy].[5]

In 1761, Haydn entered the service of Prince Esterházy, a wealthy Hungarian nobleman whose family was famous for their patronage of the arts. For nearly thirty years, Haydn was employed by the Esterházy family, and he composed the majority of his musical works while living in Esterháza, the Esterházy family's palace (during this time, Esterháza was one of the finest palaces in Europe, and even had its own opera house, and two concert halls).

Fig. 3.3 *Esterháza Palace, 1780*

Although Esterháza was somewhat isolated from Europe's musical scene (it was outside of Vienna), Haydn's reknown gradually spread throughout Europe. Following the death of Haydn's patrons (Prince Paul Anton and later his brother Prince Nikolaus), Haydn moved to Vienna and commenced entrepreneurial ventures selling his music to publishers and to individual clients.

Haydn composed his *Quartet in C major, Op. 76, No. 3* in 1797. It is known as the *Emperor Quartet* due to the fact that Haydn based the melody in the second movement on the Austrian *Emperor's Hymn*, a piece which Haydn had composed at the request of government officials (Haydn completed the *Emperor's Hymn* in early 1797). The *Emperor's Hymn* was first sung in honor of the emperor's birthday, and became so popular, that it later became the national anthem of Austria and Germany.

TECHNIQUE TIPS: This piece is an arrangement of the second movement, "Andante," from Haydn's *Emperor Quartet*. This movement is in the small form of theme and variations. In this arrangement, the theme of the *Emperor's Hymn* is stated in the first 20 measures of this piece, and then one, simplified variation of the theme is presented (in Haydn's full score of this movement, four variations of the theme are presented). The tempo of this piece is *poco adagio cantabile*, meaning it should be played with a singing style of playing, and a rather slow and leisurely tempo. Since this melody was composed in honor of the Emperor (and was also used as Austria's national anthem), play the melody in a flowing, majestic and singing manner. The simplified variation of the theme used in this arrangement (measures 21 to the end), is based on a version found in T. Mee Pattison's *Maidstone Violin Tutor*, published in London in c.1897.[6]

SECTION 3.7

PIECE: SURPRISE SYMPHONY NO. 94, 2ND MOVEMENT

Haydn composed *Symphony No. 94*, also known as the *Surprise Symphony*, in 1791. Although most of Haydn's 104 symphonies were composed while he was employed by the Esterházy family, some of his later symphonies such as the *Surprise Symphony*, were not. During the Classical Period, genres (large forms) such as symphonies, string quartets, sonatas and concertos were usually structured in multi-movement plans such as:

> *Concerto* (three movements)
>
> *String quartet and trio* (three or four movements)
>
> *Sonata* (for solo instruments or solo instrument with piano accompaniment—three or four movements)
>
> *Symphony* (four movements)

Haydn's symphonies used a four movement structure, and the inner structure of each of these movements typically used the following standardized small forms:

Typical Symphony Structure—4 movements

1ˢᵗ movement: Fast. Sonata-Allegro design.

2ⁿᵈ movement: Slow. Theme and variations, Sonata-Allegro, Rondo or Through Composed design.

3ʳᵈ movement: A dance form, such as Minuet and Trio or Scherzo (usually in triple meter).

4ᵗʰ movement: Fast. Rondo or Sonata-Allegro design

The last twelve symphonies that Haydn wrote are often called the London Symphonies; twelve symphonies that were commissioned by Johann Peter Salomon, a London violinist and concert producer. Salomon not only paid for Haydn to write the music, but he also arranged for Haydn to come to London to conduct them. It is interesting to note that the number of players in Classical period orchestras expanded during Haydn's lifetime. The size of Haydn's Esterházy orchestra was 13-24 players, a typical size for a Classical period orchestra, and probably more comparable to what would be called a chamber orchestra today. Towards the end of his career, when Haydn conducted some of his late symphonies in London, the size of orchestras playing his music had increased to 60.

Haydn composed *Symphony No. 94* in 1791, and the first performance was held in London in 1792 at one of Salomon's subscription concerts. It is nicknamed the *Surprise Symphony* because of a surprising, loud and unexpected chord in the second movement, "Andante" (this chord occurs immediately after a very quiet, pianissimo section).[7] Haydn described why he inserted this loud chord in the second movement of his *Symphony No. 94*:

> I asked him once in jest whether it was true that he had composed the Andante with the Drum Stroke [Symphony No. 94] to waken the English who fell asleep at his concert. 'No,' came the answer, 'but I was interested in surprising the public with something new; and in making a brilliant debut, so that my student Pleyel, who was at that time engaged by an orchestra in London (in 1792) and whose concerts had opened a week before mine, should not outdo me.[8]

TECHNIQUE TIPS: This arrangement of the second movement from Haydn's *Surprise Symphony* has the dynamic marking *andante* at the beginning of the music, indicating a moderately slow tempo should be used. First and second endings are also found in this movement, and these endings indicate the performer should play the first ending the first time through the music, and then return to the beginning of the piece. When playing through the music for a second time, the first ending should be skipped over, and the second ending should be played. This movement begins softly, with the dynamic marking of *p* (play softly or quietly). Another dynamic marking is found at the beginning of the piece: *pp*, and it is placed in parentheses next to the *p*, *piano* marking. This dynamic marking of *pp* indicates when the music is played through the second time, it should be played *pianissimo* (*pp*), meaning very softly. Haydn used this second *pp* dynamic marking to heighten the "surprise" of the *ff* and accent of the note in measure 9 (*ff* stands for *fortissimo*, and means the music should be very loud. An accent is indicated by the sign > and means the note should be played forcefully). Dots are also placed over some of the notes in this piece, indicating a light, crisp, slightly separated bow stroke should be used (you may want to experiment with the bowing for these sections, and decide for yourself if you want to use an on-the-string stroke such as *martelé* or *staccato*, or an off-the-string bow stroke such as *spicatto*). Beginning in measure 10, a new theme with a melody featuring slurs is presented, and a variation of the main theme returns in measure 18 to the end.

SECTION 3.8

PIECE: PASTORAL SYMPHONY NO. 6

Fig. 3.4 *Beethoven*

Ludwig van Beethoven (1770-1827) composed *Symphony No. 6* in 1806. Scholars often describe Beethoven as a composer who bridged the Classical and Romantic style periods, because he extended the Viennese Classical style of composers such as Mozart and Haydn, and expanded it in new directions, ushering in the Romantic period. Beethoven was raised in Bonn, Germany. His father was a minor musician at the court of Bonn, and Beethoven's musical education began with his father. Beethoven also received musical training from Haydn (Beethoven traveled to Vienna to study with him); Johann Georg Albrechtsberger, a leading teacher of counterpoint and composition; and Antonio Salieri, an Italian opera composer.

Beethoven did not lead an easy life. He apparently was rather eccentric and strong-willed, and gradually began going deaf when he was in his late 20s. When none of the doctor's he consulted for his hearing problems could help him, Beethoven became so despondent that he even considered suicide. The following quote comes from an unsent letter Beethoven wrote to his brothers in 1802. It is nicknamed the "Heiligenstadt Testament" because Beethoven wrote it while staying in the village of Heiligenstadt, just outside of Vienna:

> I was yet obliged early in life to isolate myself, and to pass my existence in solitude…I found it impossible to say to others: Speak louder; shout! for I am deaf!…What humiliation when anyone beside me heard a flute in the far distance, while I heard *nothing,* or when others heard *a shepherd singing*, and I still heard *nothing!* Such things brought me to the verge of desperation, and well nigh caused me to put an end to my life. *Art! art* alone,

deterred me. Ah! how could I possibly quit the world before bringing forth all that I felt it was my vocation to produce?…I joyfully hasten to meet Death. If he comes before I have the opportunity of developing all my artistic powers, then, notwithstanding my cruel fate, he will come too early for me, and I should wish for him at a more distant period; but even then I shall be content, for his advent will release me from a state of endless suffering. Come when he may, I shall meet him with courage. Farewell![9]

Despite his gradual loss of hearing, Beethoven continued composing, and some of his greatest masterpieces were created while he struggled with increasing deafness (he eventually became completely deaf). Composing music was not effortless for Beethoven. It was a strenuous ordeal, and his manuscripts with their many markings illustrate how painstaking the process was for him. Because of this, he was not as prolific a composer as others; as an example of this, Beethoven composed a total of 9 symphonies during his lifetime (Mozart composed 50 symphonies, and Haydn composed 104). Beethoven actively composed music throughout his life, and although his musical output may not have been large, his compositions were highly regarded and acclaimed.

Many scholars regard Beethoven as one of the first musicians to have had a successful career as an independent, free-lance musician. Instead of having to rely solely on patrons, Beethoven composed on commission, sold his compositions to publishers, taught music, and gave private and public concerts (he was regarded as a piano virtuoso). Although he enjoyed his independent status as a musician, his lack of a stable income caused him to constantly worry about money, and in 1809, Beethoven sought and obtained a guaranteed annual yearly salary from the Archduke Rudolph (this salaried status did not inhibit Beethoven from continuing his entrepreneurial efforts). As long as he remained in Vienna, the Archduke guaranteed Beethoven an income of 4000 florins a year, not a huge amount, but it was enough help allay Beethoven's financial fears.

Beethoven composed his *Symphony No. 6* in 1802, and titled it *Pastoral Symphony*. It is an example of program music: instrumental music which represents extra-musical concepts such as emotions, scenes or events through the music, not through words (another name for program music is descriptive music). At the time Beethoven wrote this piece, he was staying in the countryside of Vienna, and he immersed himself in nature, notebook in hand, to record his musical ideas. Beethoven provided a title to *Symphony No. 6* that illustrates how the feelings of nature inspired him in writing this piece: "The Pastoral Symphony, more the expression of feeling than painting." Beethoven's musical score includes the following descriptive phrases for each of the five movements of his *Pastoral Symphony*:[10]

First Movement: "The awakening of joyful feelings upon arriving in the country."

Second Movement: "Scene by the brook."

Third Movement: "Merry gathering of country folk."

Fourth Movement: "Thunderstorm."

Fifth Movement: "Happy, thankful feelings after the storm: shepherd's song."

(*movements 3, 4, and 5 are played continuously without the usual breaks between movements*)

TECHNIQUE TIPS: This piece is an excerpt from the first and second movements of Beethoven's *Pastoral Symphony No. 6*. Some of the instrumental techniques found in this piece are slurs, meter changes, and bow lifts. The first movement, "The awakening of joyful feelings upon arriving in the country," features a bright, lively melody. The second movement, "Scene by the brook" begins in measure 38, and has a 6/4 meter with a strong, triple pulse which depicts the sound of a flowing brook (ONE-two-three-FOUR-five-six). When you reach measures 88-89, note that although these notes are tied, a bow change is indicated (this is done so you'll end the piece on a down-bow). Try to change your bow as smoothly as possible so the notes sound like one, sustained note through the bow change.

STUDY UNIT 4—ROMANTIC MUSIC

ROMANTIC MUSIC SECTIONS

Fig. 4.1 *Paganini, 1831*

SECTION 4.1

ROMANTIC MUSICAL PERIOD OVERVIEW (1820-1900)

1) **Romanticism and emotions in music.** The term Romanticism was originally used in the late nineteenth century by literary critics to describe literature with great emotion and imagination. The term came to also define art and music which evoked great emotion, expression and feeling. During the Romantic period, the balanced logic and restraint of the Classical style of music were replaced by the emotions, subjectivity and expressive sounds of Romanticism. In order to produce these new sounds, large orchestras became commonplace, and composers experimented with exoticism, expressive harmonies, new instrumental tone colors, and supernatural and mystical topics.

2) **Nationalism and music.** During this period, music became a symbol of national pride, and many composers sought to create a distinct style of music which captured the essence of their nation's people and culture. Composers used different techniques to achieve this result, and a

few of these approaches were: making arrangements of folk music; using folk melodies and dances as the basis for a serious composition; imbuing compositions with folk music characteristics; and using programmatic elements to evoke feelings, places and history associated with their country. Many composers used their compositional techniques to elevate folk music to the level of art music, and nationalistic composers could be found in countries throughout Europe.

3) **New opportunities for musicians.** The Romantic period was a time when musicians no longer had to rely on the patronage of the aristocracy or the Church in order to earn a living. Public concerts became a source of income for many composers, and other means of financial support included commissions, music publication sales, and individual patronage. Salon concerts also became another venue for musicians to perform their works. Salon concerts were regularly held in the homes of wealthy music supporters, and invited guests often included the cultural elite and prominent members of society. Notable salons included the Mendelssohn family's Sunday morning "musicales" (music performed included the music of Felix and Fanny Mendelssohn, as well as works by other composers), and Pauline Viardot's Parisian salon concerts which featured the compositions of many of her close musician friends such as Schumann, Saint-Säens, Fauré, Chopin, Gounod, and Massenet.

During this era, musicians had new opportunities to receive musical training. Music conservatories, often run by the state, were founded in major cities such Paris (1795), Prague (1811), Vienna (1817), London (1822), Brussels (1832), Leipzig (1843), and Saint Petersburg (1861). The purpose of most of these European conservatories was to help elevate and preserve the country's musical heritage and culture, and the finest musical training was often offered at no cost to the talented students. Many of the Romantic period's most notable musicians received training at these conservatories, and music conservatories continue to play a prominent role in training professional musicians today.

4) **Program music and nature.** Nature was a popular theme of Romanticism, and composers found ways to use music to evoke the sounds and feelings of nature. Program music or descriptive music are terms used to describe instrumental music which represent extra-musical concepts such as emotions, scenes, stories or events through music, and many composers wrote program music during this era.

SECTION 4.2

ROMANTIC MUSICAL STYLE CHARACTERISTICS

Performing Medium. Chamber music ensembles, large symphony orchestras, opera companies, and piano were the predominant performing mediums during this era.

Rhythm. Rhythmic complexity and changing tempos were frequently used during the Romantic period. Some music featured strong beats, meter and rhythm, and other compositions employed fluid rhythm and meter that obscured the use of the barline. During this era, the increased technical facility of virtuoso performers led to faster tempos than prior eras.

Melody. During this period, melodies became subjective, emotional and often were virtuosic (with long runs, arpeggios and ornamentation). Greater technical proficiency by performers led to an expansion in the range of melodies and wide leaps between notes, and dynamics were frequently used to heighten the expressive nature of the music. Many composers also used folk songs or programmatic ideas as the basis for their melodies.

Harmony. Although a considerable amount of music from this period used traditional harmonies based on major and minor scales, new and complex harmonies were introduced such as the use of modulations and chromatic tones.

Texture. As in the Classical period, during the Romantic era, homophonic texture was primarily used (melody with accompaniment), and development sections sometimes used polyphonic texture.

Form. Genres used included large forms from prior eras such as concertos, sonatas, symphonies (often with programmatic titles), and operas. New forms emerged such as character pieces for piano or strings such as the nocturne, waltz, and etude. Other new forms included programmatic works such as symphonic poems and programmatic pieces.

SECTION 4.3

PIECE: HUNGARIAN DANCE NO. 5

Johannes Brahms (1833-1897), the composer of *Hungarian Dance No. 5*, was a German composer and came from a family of musicians. He began studying music at an early age, first with his father and later with teachers such as Eduard Marxsen, a prominent Hamburg pianist and composer. Brahms began his career as a musician when he was employed as a pianist to play popular music in local theaters and at eating and entertainment houses for the working class called *Schänken*. He also supplemented his income by composing arrangements for ensembles such as brass bands. These activities caused Brahms to become extremely interested in folk music, and he began compiling collections of European folksongs. His interest in folk music continued throughout his life, and one area of folk music which particularly fascinated Brahms, was the Hungarian style of gypsy music (called *style hongrois*).[1]

In 1853, Brahms went on a concert tour as an accompanist for the Hungarian violinist Eduard Remenyi. While on tour, he met notable musicians such as Franz Liszt, the prominent violinist Joseph Joachim, and Robert and Clara Schumann. Brahms developed a close friendship with the Schumann's. Brahms was invited to move to the Schumann's home to study music with Robert, and while there, he developed a close friendship with the family. When Robert Schumann was hospitalized for mental illness, Brahms stayed to assist the family, and eventually fell in love with Robert's wife, Clara. Clara was fourteen years older than Brahms, and was a gifted musician too (she was a brilliant pianist and a fine composer). When Robert died, leaving Clara free to marry, Brahms moved away, possibly frightened by the thought of losing his freedom (Clara was the mother of seven children). Although Brahms never married, he continued to express his love for Clara and her children throughout his life.

Brahms composed *Hungarian Dance No. 5* in 1868, and it was part of a set of 21 Hungarian folk dances for solo piano, four-hand (four-hand piano music is written for two pianists, using the same piano). These dances were based on Hungarian folk tunes, and the lively rhythm and pleasing melody made them very popular, particularly with amateur musicians who enjoyed playing music in their homes. Brahms later arranged ten of these dances for solo piano, but some of the most frequently performed versions of his Hungarian Dances are orchestral arrangements by other composers.[2]

TECHNIQUE TIPS: This arrangement of *Hungarian Dance No. 5* features tempo changes such as *rubato* and *ritardando* (abbreviated as *rit.*). *Rubato* is an Italian term that means means "robbed," and it refers to a temporary robbing of time by either slowing or speeding the tempo or rhythmic value of notes in a passage of music. *Ritardando* means to gradually become slower and slower. This piece is a dance, and the dots over some of the notes indicate that a *spicatto* bow stroke should be used. *Spicatto* is an off-the-string, controlled bouncing bow stroke that produces a crisp sound and very short notes. Other bowing indications include the tenuto sign, a line drawn over or under the note: _ to indicate the note should be played sustained or broadly, and held for its whole value.

This piece also has sections with repeat signs, a first and second ending, and the sign *D.C. al Coda* (*D.C.* is an abbreviation for "da capo", and means "from the beginning," and *coda* means "tail," and refers to a concluding section of a piece). A double bar with two dots is a repeat marking, and indicates the music in between the repeat signs should be repeated. First and second endings should be played as follows: play the first ending the first time through the music, and then return to the beginning of the piece. When playing through the music for a second time, the first ending should be skipped over, and the second ending should be played. Towards the end of the piece, in measure 50, there is a repeat sign and a *D.C. al Coda* marking with the added notation, 2x. This means the *D.C. al Coda* marking should not be followed until you are playing through the music for the second time (after you've repeated the section). This should be played as follows: when you reach the repeat sign in measure 50, return to the repeat marking in measure 43, and repeat the section. When you reach the *D.C. al Coda* marking in measure 50 for the second time, go back to the beginning of the piece, play to the *Coda* sign: , then jump to the *Coda* section at the end to finish the piece (beginning in measure 51). A quadruple stop, a chord using four strings, is found in the last measure of this arrangement. To play the quadruple stop, let your bow balance on the lower two strings to play the lower double stop first, then quickly roll to the upper two strings and play the upper double stop. If this is too difficult, simply play the top note of the chord.

SECTION 4.4

PIECE: "THE MOLDAU" FROM MÁ VLAST

Bedřich Smetana (1824-84) was a Czech composer and conductor, and wrote the symphonic poem "The Moldau" from *Má Vlast* in 1874. Smetana was well-known for his nationalistic compositions, and was best known for the following two nationalistic works: *The Bartered Bride*, an opera, and *Má vlast*, a cycle of six symphonic poems. Smetana was born in a small town in Bohemia (known today as the Czech Republic), the seventh child of a wealthy brewer (his father was also an amateur violinist). Smetana played the violin and piano from an early age, and began composing when he was eight.

Smetana studied music composition with Josef Proksch in Prague from 1843-47 (Proksch was noted for his progressive style of teaching, and was the founder of a Prague music school called *Musikbildungsanstalt*).[3] In addition to being a composer and a strong supporter of nationalistic Czech music, Smetana was a conductor, pianist and teacher. For over twenty years, he supported his family by teaching music, including a six year stay in Sweden, where he composed, conducted and taught. Smetana's orchestral music, particularly his symphonic poems, were influenced by Liszt (while living abroad, Smetana was befriended by Liszt).

In 1866, Smetana was appointed the conductor of Prague's Provisional Theatre, and while there, he was able to include the works of many Czech artists in the repertory played by the orchestra. Operas were also performed at the Provisional Theatre, including some by Smetana (most of his operas had a nationalistic theme and used the Czech language). Out of the eight operas Smetana completed, his most successful was *The Bartered Bride*, an opera based on folk material and Bohemian legends. Smetana also composed songs, music for orchestra and chamber ensembles, and music for piano. Many of his works were programmatic with a nationalistic theme.

Like Beethoven, Smetana became deaf towards the end of his life. He continued to compose during this time, and wrote two string quartets, his last three operas, and completed *Má vlast*, a cycle of six symphonic poems. A symphonic poem (also known as a tone poem) is a programmatic orchestral work that expresses extra musical ideas such as emotions, scenes or events through the music. *Má vlast* is an example of nationalistic music and program music, and represents Smetana's deep love for his country. Smetana employed programmatic elements in *Má vlast* to evoke the beauty of the country, legends of the past, and great moments in Bohemian history.[4][5][6]

The best known of the six symphonic poems in this cycle is the second, *The Moldau* (*Vltava*). The Moldau River is the longest river in Czechoslovakia, and flows for nearly 300 miles. It begins in the Bohemian Forest, runs through the capital of Prague, and finally empties into the Elbe River. Smetana included the following description in a program he wrote to accompany *The Moldau's* musical score:

> Two springs pour forth in the shade of the Bohemian forest, one warm and gushing, the other cold and peaceful. Their waves joyously rush down over their rocky beds, then unite and glisten in the rays of the morning sun. Coming through Bohemia's valleys, they grow into a mighty river. Through the thick woods it flows as the joyous sounds of a hunt and the hunter's horn are heard ever closer. It flows through grass-grown pastures and lowlands where a wedding feast is being celebrated with song and dance. At night, wood and water nymphs revel in its sparkling waves. Reflected on its surface are fortresses and castles—witnesses of past days of knightly splendor and the vanished glory of bygone ages. The Moldau swirls through the St. John Rapids, finally flowing on in majestic peace toward Prague to be welcomed by historic Vyšehrad [a legendary royal castle]. Then it vanishes far beyond the poet's gaze.

TECHNIQUE TIPS: This arrangement is an excerpt from *The Moldau*, and highlights programmatic features from Smetana's work. In the first two measures, the rippling sounds in the piano part evoke the sound of the source of the Moldau: two rippling springs. The rippling piano part continues throughout the piece, unifying the composition with the sound of water in motion, and the primary melody begins in measure 3. This main theme has a broad, majestic and flowing sound, and represents the Moldau River as it travels through Czecheslovokia.

The tempo marking at the beginning of this piece is *allegro comodo non agitato,* meaning the piece should be played in a fast, yet leisurely tempo that is neither too fast nor too slow, and should be performed in a manner that is not agitated or restless (*allegro* means lively and fast; *comodo* is a comfortable, leisurely tempo; and *non agitato* means not agitated). As you play this piece, use smooth bows, and when *tenuto* markings are used with slurred notes, make sure you slightly pause between the notes to slightly separate them (as in measures 4, 7, 8, 9 *etc.*). Although no dynamic markings are provided in this arrangement, you may want to experiment with different ways to musically express the mood and imagery of this piece. Note that in measure 26, a D# accidental is added to the melody in this measure only. The very last note of the piece is held for 3 measures while the bass line of the piano plays the rippling sound of the stream one final time. As you play this last note, use a down-bow, and although no additional bow markings are indicated, if you're running out of bow, try to imperceptibly and smoothly change your bow as often as needed, then end with a down bow.

SECTION 4.5

PIECE: "HALLING" FROM 25 NORWEGIAN FOLKSONGS AND DANCES

Edvard Grieg (1843-1907) was a Norwegian composer, conductor and pianist, and he composed *25 Norwegian Folksongs and Dances,* Op. 17 in 1869. Grieg was an ardent supporter of Norwegian music, and he used Norwegian folk songs and dances as the basis for many of his compositions. He was raised in a musical family, and his mother, a pianist, taught him how to play the piano. When the internationally renowned Norwegian violinist Ole Bull heard Grieg play the piano, Ole Bull strongly encouraged Grieg's parents to send their talented son to the prestigious Leipzig Conservatory. A few months later, Grieg was sent to study music at the Leipzig Conservatory (Grieg was 15 years old at the time).

Although Grieg studied with fine teachers at the Leipzig Conservatory, while he was there, his music and compositional style were largely shaped by German and Danish musicians. When Grieg was in his early 20s, he spent a summer with the violinist Ole Bull. Ole Bull was a strong advocate of Norwegian folk music, and under his tutelage, Grieg became very interested in Norwegian folk songs and Norwegian dance music (Grieg's friendship with Ole Bull continued until Ole Bull's death in 1880). Later that year, Grieg met the nationalist Norwegian musician Rikard Nordraak, and he too had an impact on Grieg's emerging interest in Norwegian nationalism. Like Grieg, Nordraak had also been influenced by Ole Bull. Nordraak's first public appearances as a musician took place when Ole Bull invited him to accompany him in concerts in1859. Nordraak later became so well-known, that he was asked to compose the Norwegian national anthem. Grieg's interactions with Ole Bull and Nordraak heavily influenced his decision to infuse his music with a Norwegian character, and Grieg did his best to help establish a distinctly Norwegian form of art music. Grieg was well known for his songs, piano music, chamber music, and orchestral music such as *Peer Gynt,* incidental music for a play by Henrik Ibsen (Grieg later extracted part of this music for two orchestral concert suites entitled *Peer Gynt Suites No. 1* and *2*).[7]

One of the instruments Grieg was intrigued by, was the Norwegian national instrument, the Hardanger fiddle. It is interesting to note that although Ole Bull helped promote the popularity of the Hardanger fiddle (and played on a Hardanger fiddle for some of his international tours), Ole Bull usually performed on his own modified violin and bow, altered after the manner of the Hardanger fiddle with a slightly shaved down bridge, and a bow longer and heavier than a traditional violin bow.[8]

The Hardanger fiddle (called *Hardingfele* in Norwegian) is a Norwegian folk instrument dating from approximately 1650, and is named for the region in which it originated (near the Hardanger fjord of Norway). Although the Hardanger fiddle has many similarities with the violin, it differs from the violin in the following ways:

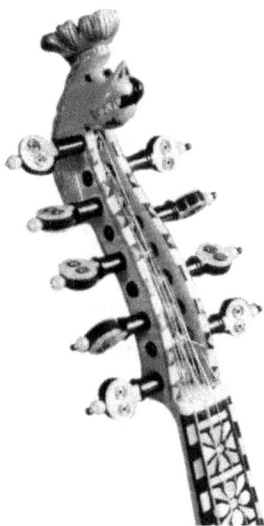

1) It is strung with two sets of strings. Like the violin, it is strung with four melodic strings, but it also has four or five sympathetic strings strung under the fingerboard that resonate and add overtones to the sound while notes are being played.

2) The fingerboard and bridge are flat (not curved like conventional violin).

3) The body and neck are slightly shorter and fatter than the conventional violin.

4) F-holes are angled.

5) The violin is decorated with bone, mother-of-pearl inlay, and black pen-and-ink drawings called "rosing." The peg box is ornately carved in a shape such as a dragon or human head.[9] [10]

Fig. 4.2 *Hardanger Scroll*

As an example of Grieg's interest in the Hardanger fiddle, the opening phrase from Grieg's *Peer Gynt Suite No. 1* ("Morning"), is said to have come from the Hardanger fiddle's sympathetic strings. It should be noted, however, that Norway has two types of folk fiddles: the Hardanger fiddle, and the regular fiddle. Chris Goertzen observed that the regular fiddle has also played a prominent role in Norway's folk song tradition, and that the fiddle's contributions to Norwegian folk music has been eclipsed by the Hardanger fiddle's distinctive appearance and unique status as a national symbol of Norway. Gortzen explained further when he said:

> The Hardanger fiddle has been intensively studied by both Norwegians and foreigners, while the fiddle has received much less scholarly attention from Norwegians and none from outsiders. The fiddle—physically the same as the violin—is played in the east, north, and in some parts of coastal Norway by as many fiddlers as devote themselves to the Hardanger

fiddle, or more. Its tradition is at least as long as that of the Hardanger fiddle, and arguably more vigorous.[11]

Grieg composed his first set of Norwegian folksong arrangements in 1869: *25 Norwegian Folksongs and Dances*, *Op. 17*, and this music was based on a collection of Norwegian folk tunes gathered by Ludvig Mathias Lindeman (1812-1887). Grieg dedicated his *25 Norwegian Folksongs and Dances, Op. 17* to Ole Bull, and one of Ole Bull's favorite pieces in this collection was purportedly the "Halling" used in this arrangement (an 1881 publication of this piece noted "Ole Bull was especially fond of this Halling, and played it frequently").[12]

TECHNIQUE TIPS: Halling is the name of a Norwegian folk dance, and it is usually in a fast, duple time (2/4 or 6/8). As a dance, the halling is danced as a solo man's dance to display strength and agility, and the dancer either kicks his foot high towards the ceiling, or kicks down a hat that is held up high.[13] The tempo of this arrangement of "Halling" is moderately fast (*moderato*), and the music should be played in a lively, vigorous manner. Some of the notes have dots over or under them, indicating they should be played with short, crisp bows. The last note of the piece is a triple stop, and to execute this bow stroke, play the bottom two notes of the chord first, then the top two notes of the chord.

SECTION 4.6

PIECE: EMPEROR WALTZ

Johann Strauss II (1825 -1899) composed *Emperor Waltz* in 1889. Strauss was an Austrian composer, conductor and violinist, and was considered to be the leading European composer of dance music of his time. Johann was a member of the famous Strauss family, and they were particularly noted for their waltz music. The waltz was the most popular ballroom dance form in the 19th century, and the Strauss family played a prominent role in Vienna's social scene, composing and performing waltzes and other dance music for dance establishments and social events. Members of the Strauss family were internationally renowned for their Strauss Orchestra performances (this orchestra was begun by Johann I, the senior member of the Strauss family). Johann Strauss II became the most famous member of the musical Strauss family, and he was awarded the nickname "The Waltz King."[14]

The waltz form, a dance with a triple meter, originated in rural dance music, and Johann Strauss I and a fellow-musician, Joseph Lanner, expanded and formalized this rural dance form. Johann Strauss II took the waltz form begun by his father and Lanner a step further, and added new melodic, harmonic and structural dimensions. Strauss II eventually elevated the waltz form beyond the ballroom and the realm of popular music, to the level of art music suitable for the concert hall. The term Viennese Waltz is sometimes used to describe the waltzes which emerged from Vienna during this time, a term which not only refers to the fully developed form of the waltz, but also to stylized elements in performing the waltz such as a subtle use of *rubato* and a slight anticipation of the second beat.[15]

Johann Strauss II composed *Emperor Waltz* (*Kaiser-Walzer*) in honor of the Austrian Emperor, Franz Josef's visit to the German Kaiser, Wilhelm II. Johann conducted the premier of this piece at the newly-opened Berlin Königsbau concert hall in 1889.[16]

TECHNIQUE TIPS: This arrangement of the *Emperor Waltz* has the flowing triple meter of a waltz, with a strong ONE-two-three pulse in each measure. Use smooth, full bows to maintain the momentum and rhythm of this waltz.

SECTION 4.7

PIECE: VIEILLE CHANSON

Fig. 4.3 *Viardot*

Pauline Viardot (1821-1910) composed "Vieille Chanson" in the 1890s. Viardot was a French singer, composer and voice teacher. Her musical works include pieces for violin and piano, operettas, and many songs for voice and piano. Viardot's birth name was Michelle Ferdinande Pauline Garcia (her married name was Viardot, thus Pauline Viardot). She was the daughter of two opera singers: Manuel Garcia, and Joaquina Garcia-Stiches. Her brother, Manuel Garcia Jr., was an opera singer, and her sister Maria Malibran was a world famous opera star (Malibran was Maria's married name, and Maria's second husband was the famous violinist Charles de Bériot). Viardot received vocal training from her parents, studied piano with Meysenberg and Franz Liszt, and composition with Anton Reicha.[17]

Viardot sang in operas such as Rossini's *Otello*, Meyerbeer's *Le prophete*, Berlioz's 1859 Paris production of Gluck's *Orfeo*, and gave Brahm's debut performance of his *Alto Rhapsody*. In 1840, she married the French writer Louis Viardot, and their Parisian home was an influential gathering place for musicians and intellectuals. Viardot followed the Parisian tradition of having a music salon. The purpose of a music salon was not only to offer entertainment, but also to feature musical works by promising composers and performers. Viardot regularly held informal salon concerts on Thursday nights and Sunday afternoons in her home (the Sunday afternoon concerts were generally reserved for close friends). Musicians such as Schumann, Saint-Säens and Fauré dedicated songs to her, and some of her close friends included Chopin, Gounod, Massenet, George Sand, and Ivan

Turgenev. Some composers even credited Viardot for helping launch their careers (musicians such as Massenet, Saint-Säens, Gounod, and Fauré).[18]

Viardot had four children: two daughters who became concert singers, a daughter who became a writer and composer (Louise Heritte-Viardot), and a son, Paul (1857-1941) who studied violin with the renowned violinist Hubert Léonard. Paul Viardot later became a conductor, composer and violinist. Viardot composed and dedicated a set of six violin and piano pieces entitled *6 Morceaux pour Piano et Violon* to her son Paul, and this work was first published in Paris by J. Hamelle in the 1890s. "Vieille Chanson" is the fifth piece in this collection of lyrical, romantic pieces for violin and piano.[19]

TECHNIQUE TIPS: "Vieille Chanson" is in a minor key, and Viardot's expressive melody and dynamic changes add to the emotional quality of this lovely piece. The intimate nature of this composition makes it likely that it was one of the pieces performed in Viardot's music salon in her home.

SECTION 4.8

PIECE: "ANDANTE" FROM VIOLIN CONCERTO IN E MINOR

Fig. 4.4 *Felix directing a musicale while Fanny watches*

Felix Mendelssohn (1809-1847), a renowned German composer, composed his *Violin Concerto in E Minor* in 1844. Mendelssohn was the son of a wealthy German banker, and was the grandson of the philosopher Moses Mendelssohn. He was raised in a highly cultured home, and Felix and his sister Fanny were both very gifted musically (they studied music with some of the leading musicians and composers in Berlin and Paris). Fanny and Felix often performed their music at Sunday morning *musicales* (concerts) held at the Mendelssohn home (they played the music of other composers too). Berlin's cultural élite, including many prominent musicians, attended these informal salon concerts. During some of these *musicales*, the Mendelssohn family even engaged a small orchestra for Felix to experiment with some of his musical ideas (by the age of 12, he had already written six symphonies).

As a side note, although Fanny was a gifted musician and composer like her brother, her family discouraged her from performing in public or publishing her music because they felt it was unsuitable for a woman to be a professional musician. When Fanny married, her husband, Wilhem Hensel, encouraged her to publish her music, and Fanny published a small amount of her compositions. Fanny wrote over 400 works, mostly piano music and lieder, and much of this music has never been published. Fanny and Felix remained close throughout their lives, and Felix often relied on her advice and support.[20]

Felix's friend, Robert Schumann, described Felix as the Mozart of the nineteenth century, and this description aptly applies because Felix wrote music that contained classical elements and refinement, combined with the warmth, lyricism and expressiveness of Romanticism. Felix composed in most of the major musical forms of his day, and he developed an international reputation, not only for his compositions, but also for his conducting. In 1835, Felix moved to Leipzig to become the conductor of the Leipzig Gewandhaus Orchestra, and he helped elevate the status of this group until it became one of the leading orchestras in Europe. While in Leipzig, he also founded the Leipzeig Conservatory, one of the most prominent European schools of music (it still is in existence today).[21]

Felix Mendelssohn wrote his *Violin Concerto in E minor, Op. 64* for his friend Ferdinand David, a renowned violinist. It took Mendelssohn a number of years to compose, and he completed the violin concerto in 1844. It was first performed in 1845 by the Gewandhaus Orchestra with David as the soloist (David was the regular concertmaster of this group). The violin concerto was received with great acclaim at its first performance, and has since become one of the most popular violin concertos in violin literature. This piece has a typical concerto form of three movements: fast—slow—fast. One of the unique features of this piece is that Felix indicated it should be played without pause (concertos generally have a slight pause between movements), thus creating the effect of a seamless, unified musical work.

TECHNIQUE TIPS: This arrangement is based on the second movement of Mendelssohn's *Violin Concerto in E minor*. The heading of this movement is "Andante," a tempo that means a moderately slow tempo (often considered to be a walking speed). The melody has an intimate, songlike feel, and like many slow movements of concertos, this movement is structured in an A-B-A form (theme A is found in measures 1-18; theme B in measures 19-26; and theme A returns in measures 27-end).

PIECE: CELLO CONCERTO IN B MINOR

Antonin Dvořák (1841-1904), a distinguished Czechoslovakian composer, wrote his *Cello Concerto in B minor, Op. 104* in 1895. Dvořák was born in Bohemia (now Czechoslovakia) in humble circumstances (his father was a butcher and an innkeeper). Dvořák received musical training locally and in nearby towns, then moved to Prague when he was 16 to study music theory, composition and organ at the Prague Organ School (at the time, organ schools were the centers for music training in Bohemia). Following graduation, he began playing the viola in a dance band, and a few years later, members of his dance band were asked constitute the core of the newly opened Provisional Theatre in Prague. Dvořák became the principal viola player of the Provisional Theatre orchestra, and notable musicians such as the composer Smetana were conductors of this group (Dvořák played under Smetana's direction).

It took Dvořák many frustrating years before he was recognized as a composer, and Brahms played a key role in helping Dvořák achieve success. Brahms took notice of Dvořák's compositions, and highly recommended them to his (Brahms') publisher. From this point on, Dvořák's works began to be widely published, performed and acclaimed. During the 1880s, Dvořák toured Europe conducting his own music, and eventually obtained the position of composition professor at the Conservatory of Prague. Dvořák was a strong proponent of nationalism, and advocated the use of traditional folk songs and other aspects of a composer's national heritage in composing classical music. Many of his works contained nationalistic Czech elements, and he received international recognition for his symphonies, chamber music, oratorios, songs and operas.

From 1892-95, Dvořák lived in the United States, serving as the director of the National Conservatory of Music (it no longer is in existence). Two of the notable works he wrote during his time in America, were his *New World Symphony* (*Symphony No. 9*) and his *Cello Concerto in B minor, Op. 104*. Dvořák composed his *Cello Concerto in B minor* in 1895, and it was premiered in London in 1896, with Dvorak conducting. His cello concerto was an enormous success at its premiere, and to this day, it remains one of the most popular cello concertos in cello literature. Dvořák's masterful use of orchestration, his exquisite melodies, and his ability to write technically brilliant and virtuosic passages for the soloist are just a few of the features that have made this concerto a classic work of art.[22]

TECHNIQUE TIPS: Dvořák's *Cello Concerto in B minor* has three movements, and this arrangement is an excerpt from the first and second movements, *Allegro* and *Andante*. It begins with the first movement's main theme (measures 1-19), followed by two excerpts from the second, slow movement. This arrangement begins with an up-bow, and slurs are used to enhance the lyrical, soaring melody of the theme from Dvorak's first movement of his cello concerto. The tempo for this movement is *allegro*, and Dvorak provided the additional musical direction *dolce e molto sostenuto*, meaning play this section sweetly and with a sustained sound.

The second, slow movement begins in measure 20, and this lovely new melody begins with the tempo marking *adagio ma non troppo,* meaning play at a slow leisurely tempo, but not too slowly. Beginning in measure 26, the second excerpt from Dvorak's second, slow movement begins, and Dvorak's musical directions for this exquisite new melody are *molto expressivo e largamente*, meaning play this section with great expression and with a large, broad and sustained tone. In this section, the melody of one of Dvorak's songs can be heard: *Leave Me Alone (Lasst mich allein)*, a song he originally wrote for voice and piano (this melody is found in the middle of the concerto's second movement, and a brief reference to this melody is also present in the third, last movement of the concerto). Dvorak used this melody in honor of his beloved sister-in-law, Josefina, who was critically ill at the time he wrote the concerto (*Leave Me Alone* was Josefina's favorite song).

SECTION 4.10

PIECE: "NOCTURNE" FROM STRING QUARTET NO. 2

Aleksandr Porfir'yevich Borodin (1833-1887) completed his *String Quartet No. 2 in D major* in 1881. Aleksandr Borodin was a Russian composer who was trained as a medical doctor, and had a career as a professor of chemistry. He was the illegitimate son of Prince Luka Stepanovich Gedianov (Gedianishvili) and was given the surname of one of his father's serfs, Borodin (Aleksandr was legally registered as the son of his father's serf, Porfiry Ionovich Borodin). Borodin's mother, Avdot'ya Konstantinovna Antonova, raised him in St. Petersburg, and through Prince Luka's financial support, they led a privileged lifestyle. Although Borodin took music lessons and showed considerable interest in music as a child, he was even more passionate about chemistry and science, and he entered medical school just before he turned the age of 17.

While in medical school, when Borodin needed a break from his studies, he composed music or played chamber music with his friends. Although the time he spent on music concerned his mentor, a chemistry professor, Borodin was able to successfully complete medical school, and he graduated from St. Petersburg's Medical-Surgical Academy in 1856 with exceptional distinction. Following graduation, Borodin worked as a medical intern for a year, then decided that his love of chemistry outweighed medicine, and he ceased to practice medicine from that point on. He successfully obtained the degree Doctor of Medicine in 1858 (his dissertation was in a chemical field), and in 1859, was sent abroad by Russia's governing board of the Medical-Surgical Academy for research studies in chemistry.

While living abroad, in addition to his work as a chemical researcher, Borodin continued his musical pastime of composing, playing chamber music with friends, and attending concerts. Although

Heidelburg, Germany was his home base, he also traveled to other places for research or pleasure such as Paris and other cities throughout Germany and Italy. He met his future wife in Germany, a Russian pianist named Yekaterina Protopopova, and he composed some of his piano and chamber music for her (they enjoyed playing chamber music together with friends). When Protopopova's doctor recommended that she move to Italy for the winter (she was being treated for tuberculosis), Borodin arranged to temporarily move there too, and he conducted his chemical research studies using labs in Italy. Borodin and Protopopova returned to Russia in 1862, and Borodin was offered a teaching position as an assistant professor of chemistry at St Petersburg's Medical-Surgical Academy (he and Protopopova were married in April, 1863). Two years later, when his chemistry mentor at the medical school retired, Borodin was promoted to the position of chair of chemistry as a full professor.[23]

In 1862, Borodin met another musician, Mily Balakirev, and Borodin soon joined Balakirev's musical circle, which included César Cui, Modest Petrovich Musorgsky, and Nikolay Rimsky-Korsakov. It is interesting to note that Balakirev was the only member of this group who was a professional musician. Nevertheless, Borodin, Balakirev, Musorgsky and Rimsky-Korsakov became known as "the mighty handful," and their nationalistic goals included the creation of a distinctly Russian school of music. Balakirev in particular, exerted a strong influence on Borodin's musical activities, and Borodin began composing a symphony under Balakirev's encouragement and guidance. Borodin later began composing additional chamber works, songs, and even an opera, but his opera, entitled *Prince Igor,* remained unfinished at the time of his death (he unexpectedly died in 1887 at the age of 54). His friend Rimsky-Korsakov enlisted the help of the musician Alexander Glazunov, and together Rimsky-Korsakov and Glazunov completed *Prince Igor* for performance and publication. Rimsky-Korsakov and Glazunov's version of Borodin's *Prince Igor* premiered in 1890 in St. Petersburg. *Prince Igor* is regarded as a significant example of historical Russian opera, and it continues to be performed by opera companies today.[24]

Although Borodin's career choice in the field of chemistry prevented him from composing numerous works, his musical output included three symphonies (at the time of his death, his third symphony was incomplete, and was later finished by Glazunov), piano music, a symphonic poem, songs and choral works, the unfinished opera *Prince Igor*, and some chamber music. His chamber music, particularly his *Quartet No. 2*, remains popular with chamber music groups today.[25]

TECHNIQUE TIPS: Borodin's *Second Quartet in D* was dedicated to his wife, and was written as a remembrance of their courtship in Heidelburg. It has four movements, and this piece is an arrangement of the third movement, "Nocturne." "Nocturne" is both lyrical and rhapsodic with a sweet and expressive melody. "Nocturne's" melody was re-used in the 1853 musical *Kismet* for the song "And This Is My Beloved," and a string orchestra arrangement of Borodin's "Nocturne" is a popular part of orchestral literature today.

Borodin's expressive markings at the beginning of "Nocturne" are *cantabile ed espressivo,* meaning play expressively in a singing, vocal style. Use smooth, flowing bows to achieve this singing style of playing. You also may want to pay attention to the eighth note rests in the piece, and consider them as if they were breaths taken by a singer (use slight pauses to create this effect).

SECTION 4.11

PIECE: ELÉGIE FOR VIOLA AND PIANO IN G MINOR

Aleksandr Konstantinovich Glazunov (1865-1936) composed *Elégie for Viola and Piano in G minor, Op. 44* in 1893. Glazunov was a Russian composer who combined serious Russian nationalism with European international styles. He began taking piano lessons when he was nine, and started composing music when he was 11. When he was 14, he began studying composition privately with the renowned Russian composer Nikolay Rimsky-Korsakov, and although Glazunov was 21 years younger than Rimsky-Korsakov, they developed a lifelong friendship. Glazunov joined Rimsky-Korsakov in numerous musical ventures, such as completing and revising Borodin's unfinished compositions.

In 1899, Glazunov was appointed as a professor at the Saint Petersburg Conservatory. He remained associated with the conservatory for the next 30 years, and was appointed director of the conservatory in 1905. In 1922, Glazunov was awarded the Russian honor of People's Artist of the Republic. Although he composed some stage and vocal works, Glazunov is primarily known for his instrumental compositions which included symphonies, concertos, orchestral music, ballet music and chamber music.[26]

TECHNIQUE TIPS: Glazunov's *Elégie for Viola and Piano* is in the key of G minor. Minor keys are sometimes used by composers to evoke a slightly sad feeling, and Glazunov's use of a minor key adds to the sweet sadness of his poignant melody. The form of this piece is an elegy, and this term is used to describe a poem or instrumental piece that laments the loss of someone who has died. The musical direction *dolce* is placed at the beginning of the piece, meaning play the piece sweetly. The melody begins on an upbeat (start with an up-bow). The tempo of this piece is *allegretto,* indicating a moderately fast tempo should be used, and the meter is in 9/8. A 9/8 meter means there are nine eighth notes in each measure, and the eighth notes are grouped into a strong triple pulse in each measure (ONE-two-three, FOUR-five-six, SEVEN-eight-nine).

Elégie triple meter

SECTION 4.12

PIECE: "BARCAROLLA" FROM VIOLA SONATA IN Bb

Henry Vieuxtemps (1820-1881), the composer of *Sonata in Bb for Viola and Piano*, was a Belgian violinist, violist and composer. Vieuxtemps was born into a musical family, and his father, an amateur violinist, began teaching him the violin at the age of four. Vieuxtemps later studied with renowned teachers such as the violinist Charles de Bériot at the Paris Conservatoire, and composition with Simon Sechter and Anton Reicha.

Vieuxtemps was invited to give violin concerts throughout Europe and the United States, and he frequently performed some of his own compositions. Vieuxtemps was very popular in Russia, and he spent five years in St. Petersburg, Russia in the service of Tsar Nicholas I as a court soloist and professor of the violin. Following his third tour to the United States, Vieuxtemps was appointed as a professor at the Brussels Conservatory. One of his pupils, Eugène Ysaÿe, later became not only a renowned violinist, but also joined the faculty at the Brussels Conservatory.[27]

Vieuxtemps' musical output primarily consisted of orchestral and chamber music for stringed instruments (most of his works were for the violin). Vieuxtemps was a fine violist too, and he composed a number of viola pieces that are still a prominent part of viola literature. Although scholars have ascertained that Vieuxtemps did concertize as a violist, little is written about his career as a violist.[28]

TECHNIQUE TIPS: Vieuxtemps wrote his *Viola Sonata in Bb*, *Op.36* in 1863. This sonata has a lush Romantic sound, and the second movement, "Barcarolla," has an exquisite, mournful melody. It is written in a minor key, and the musical directions at the beginning of the piece indicate it should be played *con melancholia,* meaning sadly.

SECTION 4.13

PIECE: AVE MARIA FROM A THEME BY J. S. BACH

Charles-François Gounod (1818-1893), a French composer, was responsible for the piece *Ave Maria from a theme by J. S. Bach.* Gounod's father was an artist and engraver for royalty, and his mother was an accomplished pianist. Gounod studied music at the Paris Conservatoire, and was the winner of prestigious musical competitions such as the *Prix de Rome* (he won the *Grand Prix de Rome* in 1839).

Gounod's musical setting of *Ave Maria* is based on the "First Prelude in C major" from *Book I of the Well-Tempered Clavier* (*BWV 846*) by Johann Sebastian Bach. Gounod composed a melody (a descant), and superimposed it on Bach's C major prelude. Although the text *Ave Maria* (a Latin prayer used by the Catholic Church), is often used with this piece, one of the first texts which Gounod used with his melody, was a poem by the French poet Lamartine. Gounod wrote this version using the Lamartine poem in 1852: *Meditation on the First Prelude of J. S. Bach* (Lamartine: *Vers sur un album*). It is likely that Gounod used the descriptive term *Meditation* to describe the reflective nature of his melody, and the peaceful, meditative feeling of the piece. Gounod arranged another version in 1853 (for violin or cello and piano), and it wasn't until 1859 that he applied the *Ave Maria* text to his music. Other words have been adapted to this melody, but the text of *Ave Maria* is one of the most popular. This piece is sometimes called *Ave Maria by Bach-Gounod* because of the contributions of both Bach and Gounod in creating this lovely work.[29]

The following quote describes what may have inspired Gounod to use the music of Bach as the basis of his piece:

> He [Gounod] was a familiar guest of two ladies of fine mind and superior talent—Mme. Viardot (Pauline A. Garcia)…and Fanny Hensel, Mendelssohn's sister, who revealed to him the beauties of Bach and Beethoven, and inspired him to transports of admiration…It was probably not long after one of these intimate recitals, in whose course Fanny Hensel introduced Gounod to Bach, that the former composed, on the harmonious weft of the first prelude in The Well-tempered Clavichord, the fine melody of the Meditation, which helped to establish his juvenile renown. This Meditation has been made into an Ave Maria, and people have gone into ecstasies over his religious feeling. This is a total misconception; this melody has been successively adapted to very different sets of words, and it was conceived quite independently of any preconception other than musical; it is a 'counter-subject' naturally emanating from Bach's prelude, in whose harmonies it was integrally contained. To disengage it, artistic insight was needed; Gounod executed this contrapuntal operation in masterly fashion; but he did it simply as an artist.[30]

TECHNIQUE TIPS: Gounod's lyrical melody is in a flowing, sustained line. Use smooth bows, slur when needed, and carefully phrase the music. Note the use of accents in measure 32. An accent is indicated by the sign **>** (placed over or under a note) and means the note should be emphasized by adding pressure with the bow. This effect is used in measure 32 to express passion and emotion.

SECTION 4.14

PIECE: SICILIENNE, OP. 78 FOR CELLO AND PIANO

Gabriel Fauré (1845-1924), the composer of *Sicilienne, Op.78* for cello and piano, was a pianist, organist, French composer and teacher. Fauré's harmonic richness and melodic innovations exerted a powerful influence on other composers, and he was particularly noted for his sensitive and graceful songs, piano and chamber music, and a large-scale work, a Requiem.

Fauré studied music at the Ecole Niedermeyer in Paris, and his teachers included Louis Niedermeyer and Camille Saint-Saëns. Fauré was one of the founders of the *National Society for French Music,* a coalition formed in support of French music. Over 150 musicians were part of this group, and just a few of the prominent musicians who were members included composers such as Saint-Saëns, César Franck, Jules Massenet, Vincent d'Indy, Edouard Lalo, Henri Duparc and Emmanuel Chabrier. Some of the objectives of the group were to promote new music, and to encourage French composers. Fauré presented many of his works for the first time at meetings of this society.

Fig. 4.5 *The Madeleine*

In addition to composing, Fauré worked as an organist at various churches such as the prominent Parisian church, the Madeleine (he was choirmaster there too). Fauré later became a professor of composition at the Paris Conservatoire, and he became director of the conservatoire in 1905. Many of his students later became renowned French composers such as: Nadia Boulanger, Maurice Ravel, George Enescu and Charles Koechlin. In 1920, the government of France honored Fauré for his significant influence on French music by awarding him with the *Grand-Croix of the Légion d'Honneur* (musicians rarely receive this award. The *Légion d'Honneur* is the highest decoration in France, and the *Grand-Croix* is the highest degree of this award).

It wasn't until Fauré was in his 50s, that his music became widely known. Up until that time, much of his music was considered too modern to be heard in regular concert halls. His music was, however, praised by the musical elite favoring *avant-garde* French music. One of Fauré's biggest proponents was Pauline Viardot, and she frequently featured his music in her salons (he dedicated some of his works to the Viardots, and at one point, was engaged to Marianne Viardot, Pauline's daughter. Marianne ultimately called off the wedding and Fauré purportedly was heart-broken). Fauré was considered a transitional composer, one who blended the emotion and expressiveness of Romanticism with the experimental avant-garde of the 20th century in his own unique language.[31]

Fauré originally composed the piece *Sicilienne* as part of incidental music he wrote in 1893 for the French playwright Molière's play *Le bourgeois gentilhomme*. In 1898, Fauré reused *Sicilienne* when he composed incidental music for the English translation version of Maeterlinck's play *Pelléas et Mélisande*. Fauré later extracted four of the seventeen pieces written for *Pelléas et Mélisande*, and formed an orchestral suite for concerts, *Pelléas et Mélisande Suite, Op. 80* (*Sicilienne* was one of the pieces Fauré selected for this orchestral suite). Fauré's *Sicilienne* is the most popular piece from the *Pelléas et Mélisande Suite*, and it is frequently played by major orchestras today. In 1898, Fauré also scored *Sicilienne* for cello and piano, and this version is catalogued as *Op. 78*.[32]

TECHNIQUE TIPS: This piece is an arrangement of Fauré's *Sicilienne, Op.78* for cello and piano. 17th and 18th century composers frequently used the *sicilienne*, a dance, as the musical form for instrumental movements. In the 19th and 20th centuries, composers such as Fauré used the *sicilienne* to musically convey melancholy emotions or pastoral scenes. In this musical form, an upbeat was frequently used to begin melodic phrases. Although *siciliennes* generally utilize a slow 6/8 or 12/8 meter, this simplified arrangement of Fauré's piece has a 3/4 meter (the duration of the notes was doubled to make the music easier to sight-read). This piece also has numerous accidentals. An accidental is a sign such as a flat, sharp or natural indicating a momentary departure from the key signature. Accidentals apply to the note immediately following the symbol, and remain in effect throughout the measure in which it appears. In measures 43 and 44, the accidentals are enclosed with parentheses (a Bb in measure 43, and an Eb in measure 44). These are called courtesy accidentals, and are sometimes used in sheet music to remind the musician of the correct pitch after accidentals have been used in prior measures.[33]

SECTION 4.15

PIECE: "MEDITATION" FROM THAÏS

Fig. 4.6 *Jules Massenet*

Jules Massenet (1842-1912), a French composer, composed "Meditation" from *Thaïs* in 1894. Massenet was one of the most prominent French composers of opera in the late 19th and early 20th centuries. He studied music at the Paris Conservatoire, and in 1863, was the winner of the prestigious *Prix de Rome*. Winning this award enabled Massenet to study in Italy for two years, and he met the composer Franz Liszt while there (Liszt introduced Massenet to his future wife). When Massenet returned to Paris, he was commissioned to compose an opera for Opéra-Comique, and from this point on, he commenced a successful career as a composer. Massenet soon joined with other young composers who shared his musical views, and became part of a group called the *National Society for French Music*, a coalition formed to support French composers and promote French music. In addition to writing operas, Massenet composed orchestral suites, incidental music for plays, ballet music, and choral works such as oratorios, cantatas, and sacred and secular songs.

Massenet participated in Pauline Viardot's music salon concerts, and considered her a close friend. Pauline Viardot promoted and sang the leading role in his oratorio *Marie-Magdeleine.* This piece, along with another oratorio (*Eve*) and some orchestral pieces, led to Massenet being awarded France's prestigious *Légion d'honneur* in 1876. In 1878, he began teaching composition at the Paris Conservatoire.[34] In the late 1870s, Massenet's operas began attracting international fame, and he soon was regarded as one of the most illustrious French opera composers of his day. His operas were regularly performed by major operatic companies in cities such as London, Milan, and Vienna, and some of his most popular operas were *Manon* (1884), *Werther* (1892), and *Thaïs* (1894).[35][36]

Thaïs is based on Anatole France's novel, and tells the story of a young priest who seeks the salvation of a woman of questionable virtue, a courtesan named Thaïs. The piece "Meditation," is a dramatic interlude in the middle of the second act of Massenet's opera. During this interlude, when the curtains close, "Meditation" is played by a solo violin with orchestral accompaniment. The lyrical, expressive melody of this piece symbolizes the inner struggle of Thaïs as she meditates and reflects upon the direction of her life. As the piece progresses, the music's dramatic tension and soaring melody depict a spiritual awakening as Thaïs decides to change her ways and convert to Christianity. The opera *Thaïs* was premiered in Paris in 1893, but did not achieve measurable success until it was performed in Italy in 1903. From that point on, *Thaïs* has been a standard and popular part of operatic literature throughout the world.[37]

TECHNIQUE TIPS: The piece "Meditation" is extremely popular as a solo musical number (it is often used as an encore number by concert artists). Massenet used several musical terms to enhance the expressive performance of this piece. At the beginning of "Meditation," Massenet used the musical expression *andante religioso*, meaning play in a moderately slow and devotional or religious manner. *Molto sostenuto* is also indicated at the beginning of the piece, meaning play with a very sustained sound. Tempo variations are used throughout the piece such as *rall.* (*rallentando*), indicating gradually become slower and slower; *a tempo*, meaning return to the original tempo; and variations such as *a tempo piu mosso,* indicating a slightly more rapid version of the original tempo should be used. In measure 23, Massenet used the term *poco a poco appassionato*, meaning little by little, play with passion and intense feeling. He reused a variation of this term beginning in measure 30 with the expressive marking *poco piu appassionato*, meaning play slightly more passionately and with intense emotion or feeling. Beginning in measure 32, Massenet's expressive marking, *piu mosso agitato*, means play a little faster and in a slightly agitated manner. Other musical markings in the score include *calmato*, meaning play calmly. Notice the dynamic markings throughout the piece, and as you follow them, see if they assist you in interpreting the piece musically. Some of these terms include *cresc.,* an abbreviation for *crescendo* which means gradually become louder (also indicated by the marking ⟨‾‾‾⟩), and *dim.* or *diminuendo*, a term which means gradually become softer, and has the same meaning as the musical marking for *decrescend*: ⬎. When you reach measure 32, *piu mosso agitato* and *sforzando* are marked at the beginning of the next four measures. To execute this section, press into the string with your bow and play these measures intensely. When there are *tenuto* markings __ such as in measures 30-31 or parts of measures 35-36, try to use a full bow and a singing tone. There are many ways to musically express yourself as you play this piece, and you may want to experiment with the balance you like best as you play Massenet's beautiful piece, "Meditation."

SECTION 4.16

PIECE: "HABANERA" FROM CARMEN

Georges Bizet (1838-1875), a French composer and pianist, composed the opera *Carmen* in 1874. Bizet came from a musical family, and was admitted to the Paris Conservatoire a few weeks before he turned ten. While there, his teachers included Pierre Zimmerman and Charles Gounod. As a note of explanation, although Gounod was not an official teacher at the Conservatoire, he happened to be married to Zimmerman's daughter, Anna, and often substituted for the ailing Zimmerman. Both teachers saw great potential in Bizet, and Gounod even asked Bizet to assist him with musical projects (Bizet worked as an arranger on Gounod's *First Symphony*). Bizet developed a close friendship with Gounod and regarded him as an influential mentor. In 1857, Bizet won the Conservatoire's most prestigious competition, the *Prix de Rome*, which enabled him to spend almost three years in Italy, leisurely traveling, absorbing the music and culture of the Italian people, and composing.

When Bizet returned from Italy, he began to receive commissions for operas and theater music. His first major opera, *The Pearl Fishers,* was not well-received when it premiered in 1863. Bizet continued composing operas and other music such as incidental music for Alphonse Daudet's play *L'arlésienne*. When the drama was first performed in October, 1872, it had a disappointing reception. Bizet quickly extracted four pieces, scored them for full orchestra, and presented them in a concert version orchestral suite in November, 1872. It was an immediate success, and his orchestral suite *L'arlésienne* remains popular to this day.[38]

Although Bizet composed in a variety of musical genres such as orchestral and chamber music, piano music, and choral works such as oratorios, masses and sacred and secular songs, his primary focus as a composer was opera. Bizet left approximately 30 finished, incomplete or projected operas at the time of his early death at the age of 36. He is best known today for his opera *Carmen*. *Carmen* was not well-received when it premiered in Paris in March 1875. The plot, set in a Spanish atmosphere, focused on passion, betrayal, and ended with the death of the heroine, Carmen, when she was murdered by her ex-lover. The French critics labeled Bizet's *Carmen* as "immoral." Even though *Carmen* was performed 45 times during the year of its premiere, it was not considered a success until October, 1875 when it was produced in Vienna and received acclaim for performances there. From that point on, *Carmen* began to achieve international praise, and it remains one of the

Fig. 4.7 *Carmen poster, 1875*

most popular operas performed today. Unfortunately, Bizet never knew how successful his opera would become. He died of a heart attack in June, 1875, just three months after *Carmen* premiered in Paris.[39] [40]

TECHNIQUE TIPS: This piece is an arrangement of Bizet's "Habanera," one of the musical numbers from the opera *Carmen*. Bizet based "Habanera" on a Spanish song called *El arreglito*. Bizet thought *El arreglito* was a Spanish folksong, and when he learned it actually had been composed by the Spanish composer Sebastián Yradier, Bizet gave Yradier credit in the score.

The Afro-Cuban habanera rhythm plays a prominent part in Bizet's "Habanera." Try to capture the lively habanera rhythm in your playing. When you see slurred notes with a dot over or under them, this indicates slurred, martelé bowing should be used (another name for this bowing technique is slurred staccato). Martelé is a French

Habanera Rhythm

term meaning hammered. Each note is percussive, and commences with a sharp accent or "pinch" at the beginning of the note, followed by a quick release. To achieve this effect, before you set your bow in motion, apply a "pinch" or "bite" for articulation. There also are tenuto signs, a line drawn over or under the note:__ to indicate the note should be played in a sustained or broad manner, and held for its whole value. Make sure that your smooth, tenuto triplet bow strokes contrast with the pinch of the martelé bowing. Although most pieces end with a down-bow, this arrangement ends with an up-bow flourish. You may want to experiment with ending the piece with a down-bow and then an up-bow, and decide which bowing you prefer.[41]

SECTION 4.17

PIECE: "REED FLUTES" FROM THE NUTCRACKER SUITE

Peter Ilyich Tchaikovsky (1840-1893), a prominent Russian composer, wrote *The Nutcracker Suite* in 1892. Although he loved his music studies as a child, when Tchaikovsky was ten, he attended the St. Petersburg School of Jurisprudence to study a more practical subject: law. During law school, Tchaikovsky continued his musical training by taking private lessons with voice and piano teachers, and by participating in the school's cultural activities and choral instruction. When Tchaikovsky was 19, he graduated from law school and began working for the Ministry of Justice. A few years later, Tchaikovsky decided that music was more important to him than law, and he abandoned his legal career and returned to school when he was 22, this time as a music student at the St. Petersburg Conservatory of Music. Tchaikovsky studied music theory and composition with the renowned pianist and composer Anton Rubenstein (1829-1894). Three years later, Tchaikovsky graduated from the St. Petersburg Conservatory of Music, and he was asked to teach music at the Moscow Conservatory of Music. Tchaikovsky taught composition at the conservatory for 12 years while he continued to compose and produce some of his own works. He longed to compose full-time, and Tchaikovsky was granted this privilege through the financial largesse of a wealthy widow who was supportive of his music career, Nadezhda von Meck. Although they never met, Meck provided Tchaikovsky with financial assistance for 13 years.

With Meck's financial support, Tchaikovsky was free to compose full-time and travel. For the next six years, he traveled extensively to countries throughout Europe. Although Tchaikovsky used many Russian stylistic elements in his music, his compositions were also influenced by the styles of other countries, and he incorporated elements of Italian opera, French ballet, and German Romanticism into his cosmopolitan style. Tchaikovsky developed an international reputation, and his music became popular throughout Europe and the United States. Tchaikovsky was a prolific composer in most of the major genres of his time, including orchestral works such as symphonies and tone poems; concertos; chamber music; piano music; operas; choral music (sacred and secular music); songs; and ballets.

The music Tchaikovsky composed for *The Nutcracker* is one of his best known compositions for ballet. He based his music on E.T.A. Hoffmann's fairy tale, *The Nutcracker and the Mouse King*. The end result was a fairy tale ballet in two acts, and it was completed in 1892. Prior to the ballet's premier, Tchaikovsky selected eight of *The Nutcracker* pieces and compiled them into an orchestral suite designed for concert performance. *The Nutcracker Suite, Op. 71a*, was first performed in March, 1892 in St. Petersburg and was an immediate success (the ballet premiered later in December, 1892).[42]

TECHNIQUE TIPS: This piece is an excerpt from *The Nutcracker Suite's* "Dance of the Reed Flutes." Tchaikovsky titled this piece "Dance of the Mirlitons" (*mirliton* is a French term meaning a toy reed flute with a kazoo-like sound). This arrangement includes dots over or under the notes, indicating that the bow stroke *spicatto*, an off-the-string, controlled bouncing bow stroke should be used. Experiment with which section of your bow you prefer to produce the light, crisp sound of *spicatto*. A slight slowing down (*poco rit.*) is indicated in measure 8, then the term *a tempo* is used to indicate a return to the regular tempo in measure 9.

D.C. al Coda is also marked in the score. This means, when you reach the *D.C. al Coda* marking, go back to the beginning of the piece, play to the *Coda* sign: ⊕ , then jump to the *Coda* section to finish the piece. Grace notes are also found in the score. Grace notes are used to ornament the notes, and indicate the musician should quickly play the grace note, then the note to which it is attached (the grace note is not part of the rhythmic value).

Grace Note

STUDY UNIT 5—20TH CENTURY MUSIC

20TH CENTURY MUSIC SECTIONS

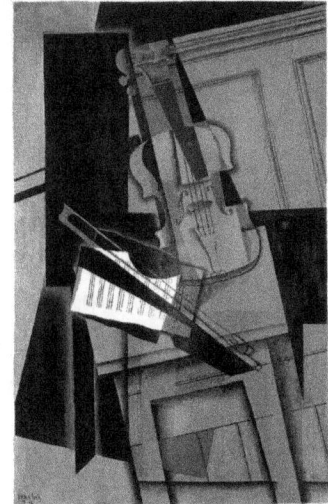

Fig. 5.1 The Violin, 1917

SECTION 5.1

20TH CENTURY MUSICAL PERIOD OVERVIEW (1900-present)

1) **World Wars and experimentation in music.** Many significant historical and political events have taken place since this era began, including two world wars. The upheavals of these times have caused composers to take many different directions, including new forms of musical expression. Some of these new forms include the following 20th century styles of music.

   a) **Impressionism.** This term describes a form of music in which new sounds and sonorities are used to convey fleeting impressions, movement and moods. Forms often used in Impressionistic music include symphonies and smaller character pieces such as preludes and nocturnes.

   b) **Expressionism**. This style of music is exemplified by compositional techniques such as twelve-tone music and serialism. The twelve tone technique, developed by the composer Arnold Schoenberg (1874-1951), refers to a system where the composer arranges the twelve notes of the chromatic scale in a fixed order. This ordered sequence of the twelve notes is called a twelve-tone row or series that forms a unique melody. Composers using this method generally would not repeat any note in the tone row until the entire series of twelve notes had been heard. Variations to the tone row include retrograde, inverted and transposed versions of the tone row. Twelve-tone music often is highly atonal, and has been used with music forms such as quartets in unconventional ways. The twelve-tone technique was later called serialism, and continues to be used by some composers today.

c) **Chance Music.** In this form of music, indeterminancy is used in the composition of the music, performance, or both. The result is a new piece of music each time the chance music is performed (chance music is also called aleatory music).

d) **Electronic music.** A few of the various forms of electronic music include: electronically produced sounds (*e.g. music concrete* which uses manipulated real sounds from a tape recorder); computer generated pitches, sounds, textures and compositions (including microtonal music); and combinations of traditional instruments with computer generated music.

2) **Past musical styles and forms have remained in use.** Musical forms and styles from previous musical periods have also been used during this era, often in experimental ways such as Post-Romantic, Neo-Classic and Neo-Baroque styles. Additionally, early music groups have been formed to perform the music of past eras such as the Baroque and Classical periods, often using authentic performance practices and period instruments.

3) **Popular music has increased in importance.** During this era, art music acquired the status of an elite form of entertainment that many members of the general public could no longer relate to. Popular music such as jazz, country, rock, pop, rap, hip-hop and other contemporary forms of popular music have become the predominant music listened to by the general public. Whereas in the past, classical music was the popular music of its day, this no longer is true.

4) **New Directions.** All sounds, styles and forms of music are now possible for composers, listeners and musicians, including the music of non-western cultures. Composers are writing both highly sophisticated and complex art music, often understandable only to an elite few, as well as art music accessible to the masses, such as music composed for movies and musical theater. Although the attendance at public classical music concerts may be waning in some cities, the core of classical music supporters remains strong. A rising tide of musical amateurs, eager to learn how to play musical instruments and to perform classical music has also emerged in recent years. Traditional modes of musical instruction and printed sheet music are plentiful, and new directions in technology such as online learning and immediate access to digital sheet music and recordings offer abundant opportunities for lifelong learning and active music making.

SECTION 5.2

20TH CENTURY MUSICAL STYLE CHARACTERISTICS

Performing Medium. Performing groups during this era include chamber orchestras; instrumental ensembles; orchestras; choral groups; computer generated instruments (including synthesizers); and mixed media (taped sounds with traditional instruments).

Rhythm. Complex, individual rhythms are used, and new rhythms and meters are common such as polyrhythms and polymeters.

Melody. Melodies are often fragmented, dissonant and experimental. Depending on the form or style used, melodies could be based on scales from non-Western countries, chromatic scales, twelve-tone rows, or microtonal scales.

Harmony. Harmony is often experimental and dissonant. Instead of all harmony being based on the interval of a third (tertian harmony, used in much of Western tonal music), harmony is sometimes based on seconds, fourths and fifths (respectively, secondal, quartal, and quintal harmony). Atonality, meaning an absence of tonality, is present in music such as twelve-tone compositions.

Texture. Polyphonic textures are often used (twelve-tone music often uses homophonic texture), and music such as impressionism or aleatory music experiment with new textures using layers of different sounds.

Form. Musical forms from previous musical periods are used, often in experimental ways. \

SECTION 5.3

PIECES: "OVERTURE" FROM PULCINELLA BALLET
AND "MODERATO" FROM SONATA NO. 1 IN G MAJOR

Igor Fyodorovich Stravinsky (1882-1971) composed *Pulcinella*, a ballet, in 1919-20. Stravinsky was a Russian composer who experimented with a wide range of compositional styles. His innovative musical ideas have caused many music scholars to regard Stravinsky as one of the most influential composers of the 20th century. He was raised in a musical family with a mother who played piano, and a father who was a highly acclaimed bass baritone, and sang with the Imperial Opera in St. Petersburg. Although Stravinsky was very interested in music (he studied piano and theory lessons from well-known teachers), he followed a traditional path towards a career in civil service and enrolled in law school at the St. Petersburg University. While he was still in law school, he continued his music studies and began studying music composition privately with Nikolay Rimsky-Korsakov. Stravinsky was influenced by Rimsky-Korsakov's nationalistic views on music, and many of Stravinsky's early compositions were nationalistic and reflected Stravinsky's interest in his Russian heritage.

Stravinsky's music attracted the attention of the Russian impresario (similar to a producer) of Ballet Russe, Sergey Diaghilev (1872-1929). Diaghilev commissioned Stravinsky to write music for five ballets. As an example of Stravinsky's impact on the music world, the third ballet he wrote for Diaghilev, *The Rite of Spring*, caused a near riot at its premiere in Paris in 1913. Stravinsky's primitivistic music, extreme dissonances, driving, unpredictable rhythms and loud orchestral effects were more than many in the audience could tolerate (contributing factors to the audience's shocked response included the primitive, angular moves of the dancers, and a plot which revolved around spring festivities in pagan Russia, ending with the violent sacrifice of a young girl to the god of spring). Interestingly enough, Stravinsky's music received a very positive response a year later, when *The Rite of Spring* was presented as an orchestral concert in Paris. Instead of fighting and booing as the audience did during the premiere of the ballet, the audience stood and cheered at the conclusion of the concert.[1] Since then, *The Rite of Spring* has become a regular and popular part of orchestral concerts and dance performances, and is widely regarded as a masterpiece of innovation.

Fig. 5.2 *Stravinsky*

Following the outbreak of World War I, Stravinsky moved to Switzerland, and when the Russian Revolution took place, Stravinsky moved to France (while there, he became a citizen of France. In later years, he also became a citizen of the United States). In 1919, Diaghelev approached Stravinsky with an idea for a another ballet: a ballet using music and dance traditions from the past, based on the music of an eighteenth century composer named Giovanni Battista Pergolesi. Diaghelev said he had collected copies of Pergolesi's music while visiting Italian music conservatories, and asked Stravinsky to orchestrate some of this music for the new ballet.

Stravinsky used the music Diaghelev gave him, and went to the British Museum to acquire additional Pergolesi music for the ballet. Stravinsky's finished work, music for the ballet *Pulcinella*, was composed in a Neo-Classic style. Neoclassicism may be defined as a 20th century composition which utilizes styles and forms of pre-Romantic music, especially those by composers from the eighteenth century such as Haydn, Bach, and Mozart. Instead of simply re-orchestrating the Pergolesi pieces he'd been given, Stravinsky reshaped and recreated the music in a style uniquely his own. He scored it for a chamber orchestra of 33 players (comparable to the small size of orchestras used during the Classical period), and intertwined the existing melodies and bass lines with modern harmonies, rhythmic modifications (such as off-beat accents), and creative orchestration. His insertion of slight dissonance into the harmonies gave it an ironic touch, and the resulting work apparently was not what Diaghilev expected.[2] Stravinsky described Diaghilev's reaction to his music for Pulcinella: "A stylish orchestration was what Diaghilev wanted, and nothing more, and my music so shocked him that he went about for a long time with a look that suggested the Offended Eighteenth Century."[3]

Pulcinella premiered at the Paris Opera House in May, 1920, and it was very well received by the public. Critics, however, were divided in their reaction to the music. The younger generation of musicians loved it, but some of the more traditional musicians and academics questioned Stravinsky's tampering with Pergolesi's original music by adding new harmonies and effects such as metric displacements. Stravinsky later extracted eleven movements from *Pulcinella* and arranged them as a concert suite. The resulting work, *Suite from Pulcinella*, was first performed in Boston in 1922, and was an immediate success. *Suite from Pulcinella* continues to be widely performed by major orchestras today.[4]

Since the time that Stravinsky composed *Pulcinella*, musicologists have determined that out of the 21 movements in *Pulcinella* once attributed to the music of Pergolesi, only 9 of these pieces were actually composed by Pergolesi.[5] For example, Stravinsky's *Overture to Pulcinella* was once thought to have been based on Pergolesi's "Sonata No. 1 in G" from his *Twelve Sonatas for Two Violins and a Bass*. Scholars have now determined that this instrumental music was actually composed by a mid-18th century Italian composer and violinist named Dominico Gallo, therefore Stravinsky's *Pulcinella Overture* was based on the first movement from Gallo's "Sonata No. 1 in G." As a note of explanation, it is likely that Pergolesi's name was applied to Gallo's composition to enhance sales of the music (Pergolesi was a better known composer than Gallo).[6]

One scholar analyzed the likely Pergolesi music Stravinsky would have had access to, and concluded that the 21 movements in *Pulcinella* were based on the music of 5 composers: Domenico Gallo (7 pieces); Carlo Monza (2 pieces); Alessandro Parisotti (1 piece); Count Unico Wilhelm van Wassenaer (1 piece); and Giovanni Battista Pergolesi (10 pieces—note this differs from the research of other Pergolesi scholars who determined that only 9 movements in Pulcinella were by Pergolesi).[7] Pergolesi scholars have also found that over ninety percent of all music attributed to Pergolesi was written by others.[8] For example, the most complete edition of Pergolesi's works was once was considered to be a collection of 148 works by Pergolesi entitled *G. B. Pergolesi: Opera omnia*, edited by F. Caffarelli, and published in Rome 1939-42. Pergolesi scholars have found that only 30 of the 148 works in *Opera omnia* were actually composed by Pergolesi. Contemporary research on Pergolesi's works is ongoing, and a research coalition (The Pergolesi Research Center), dedicated to publishing a complete and accurate collection of Pergolesi's compositions, has already compiled several volumes of his actual works.[9] [10]

Stravinsky moved to the United States in 1939, and began experimenting with more compositional styles including older forms of music (Medieval and Renaissance music), and abstract forms such as twelve-tone music (serialism). Towards the end of Stravinsky's life, he frequently used a complex system of composition that utilized rotation grids of various twelve-tone row combinations, and combined the music with sacred texts. Stravinsky's creative innovations in music continued until his death at the age of 89.[11]

TECHNIQUE TIPS: This arrangement of Stravinsky's "Overture" from *Pulcinella* is derived from Stravinsky's 1920, London publication of his vocal score: *Pulcinella Ballet in One Act for three solo voices*. If you would like to see and hear for yourself some of the ways Stravinsky reshaped Gallo's original work, an arrangement is also provided of Domenico Gallo's first movement from his *Sonata No. 1 in G Major* (Stravinsky based his overture on this movement). As mentioned earlier, although this trio sonata was originally attributed to Giovanni Battista Pergolesi, it is now known to have been composed by Gallo, a mid-18th century Italian composer and violinist. Although there are very few differences between the melodies of the two pieces (Stravinsky made minimal changes to Gallo's melody), see if you can tell the differences between these two arrangements as you play the melody along with the piano accompaniment or recording of each piece. Some of the variations Stravinsky used to change the feel of Gallo's original trio sonata included minor changes in the rhythm and meter, and slight dissonances in the harmony.

SECTION 5.4

PIECE: "ASSEZ VIF" FROM STRING QUARTET IN F MAJOR

Fig. 5.3 *Ravel*

Maurice Ravel (1875-1937), a French composer, wrote his *String Quartet in F Major* in 1903. Ravel began piano lessons when he was 7 years old, took harmony lessons when he was 12, and was admitted to the Paris Conservatoire when he was 14 years old. While there, some of his teachers included Charles-Wilfrid Bériot, Emile Pessard, André Gédalge and Gabriel Fauré. Although Ravel won second place in the prestigious *Prix de Rome* competition, first place eluded him. Between 1900 and 1905, Ravel tried to win this award five times. After his last unsuccessful effort, music critics, his teachers and friends were so outraged by Ravel's unfair treatment in the competition, that the controversy led to the resignation of the director of the Paris Conservatoire. This incident, known as the "Affaire Ravel" uncovered the fact that all of the previous competition finalists were pupils of the same professor who also happened to be a prominent member of the competition's jury.[12] [13]

Ravel began writing his only string quartet in 1903 while he was still a student at the Paris Conservatoire (he submitted the first movement of this quartet in his fourth unsuccessful attempt to win the *Prix de Rome* competition). Ravel's *String Quartet in F* was premiered in 1904, and although it was well received, some musicians gave it mixed reviews. Ravel dedicated the quartet to one of his teachers, Gabriel Fauré, but Fauré found fault with the last movement (Fauré felt it was too short). Other musicians such as Debussy praised Ravel's quartet, and it has remained popular to this day.

Ravel was influenced not only by his professors at the Paris Conservatoire, but also by the musical and intellectual environment of Paris. He acknowledged the impact of events such as the 1889 Paris World Exhibition, where he was exposed to the sounds of exotic instruments such as the Javanese gamelan and performances of Rimsky-Korsakov's nationalistic Russian music. Ravel also experimented with musical styles such as Impressionism. Impressionism began as an artistic movement, and was used to describe a style of art which was designed to convey an impression rather than a literal depiction of a scene (*e.g.* art by Impressionist painters such as Claude Monet). This term was applied to music, particularly to compositions written by French composers in the early 20th century such as Debussy and Ravel. Impressionism in music sought to convey subtle impressions, moods and emotions through compositional techniques such as new chord combinations, sonorities and harmonies, colorful instrumentation, and exotic scales.

In 1912, Ravel was commissioned by Diaghilev to write *Daphnis et Chloé* for the Ballet Russe, and was later asked by Diaghilev to collaborate with Stravinsky to orchestrate Modest Musorgski's opera *Khovanshchina* (Stravinsky and Ravel had already met in 1909, but through their work together in 1913 for Musorgski's opera, they developed a close and lifelong friendship). Throughout his career, Ravel found ways to use Classical elements of structure and form, even as he explored additional approaches to composition such as modality, bitonality, elements of exoticism from other cultures, blues, and jazz. Some of the genres Ravel composed in included orchestral music, ballet, opera, songs, piano music and chamber music. After Debussy died in 1918, Ravel was considered by many to be France's leading composer. In 1920, France even offered Ravel the decoration of the *Légion d'Honneur*, but he refused to publicly accept this honor.[14]

TECHNIQUE TIPS: Ravel's *Quartet in F* demonstrates his skillful ability to use classical form and structure to present unified melodies and themes, complex rhythmic patterns, and a wide range of tone colors and textures. The excerpt selected for this piece is an arrangement of Ravel's second movement from his *Quartet in F,* "Assez Vif " (*assez vif* is French for "rather fast"). A few of the features in this movement include *pizzicato*, *tremolo*, key changes, and triplets.

The following is a brief explanation of some of the techniques needed to play this music: *pizzicato* and *tremolo*. Pizzicato (often abbreviated as *pizz.*) is a string instrument musical direction indicating that the string should be plucked with the finger instead of being bowed. String players generally use their right forefinger (index finger) to pluck the string, and before doing so, often place their right thumb against the right corner or side of the fingerboard to support their hand while plucking the string (cellists put their right thumb against the right side of the fingerboard). When plucking the string, try to pull the string sideways so it does not snap against the fingerboard (a specific type of pizzicato which does call for the string to be plucked forcefully so it snaps against the string is called "snap pizzicato" or "Bartok pizzicato" since Bartok frequently employed this technique in his string music). A return to bowing is usually indicated by the term *arco*.

Tremolo means rapidly repeating a single note or chord. On stringed instruments, a tremolo may either be bowed or fingered. Bowed tremolo indicates the note should be played with very short, rapid and unaccented bow strokes, moving the bow back and forth for the duration of the note value. Tremolos are either measured (a subdivision of the note's rhythmic value) or unmeasured (play the note as fast as possible). Tremolo signs are indicated by short slanted lines through note stems. For example, one line through a stem indicates the bowed tremolo should be played using eight notes, two lines mean sixteenth notes, and three lines mean unmeasured tremolo. If tremolos are placed on a beamed note, the beam counts as one of these lines.

*Unmeasured
bowed tremolo*

*Unmeasured
fingered tremolo*

Fingered tremolos are played between more than one note (this is also known as slurred tremolo). Instead of the bow rapidly moving, the fingers rapidly alternate between two notes while the bow smoothly plays. Fingered tremolo is generally notated with incomplete beams placed between two notes to indicate the rhythmic value of the tremolo.

Although Ravel did use fingered tremolo in the second movement of his quartet, this arrangement has been simplified and does not include fingered tremolo. The only type of tremolo used in this arrangement is unmeasured bowed tremolo. To execute this bow stroke, use short, unaccented bow strokes in the upper third or tip of your bow. You may want to use a flexible wrist as you play the notes as fast as possible.

The title of this piece indicates that the music should be played "rather fast" (*assez vif*), and it should also be played very rhythmically. The small musical form that Ravel used for this movement is a *scherzo*. The term *scherzo* literally means "joke." As a small form in music, *scherzos* were typically used as the second or third movement of a symphony or quartet (in place of the minuet), and often were in a quick triple meter with a vigorous rhythm and a sharply contrasting harmony. Ravel's "Assez vif" definitely features these characteristics.

SECTION 5.5

PIECE: "SEHR LANGSAM" FROM 4 PIECES, OP. 7

Anton Webern (1883-1945), an Austrian composer and conductor, composed *Four Pieces for Violin and Piano, Op. 7* in 1910. When Webern was young, he studied the piano, cello and music theory, and composed in his spare time. He attended the University of Vienna to work towards a doctorate in musicology, and in 1904, as he neared the completion of his degree, he began studying music composition privately with Arnold Schoenberg (1874-1951).

Webern was heavily influenced by Schoenberg, and under Schoenberg's guidance, Webern began to undertake new directions in his compositional technique. Webern favored music which was the opposite of the grandiose, lush sounds of Romanticism. He began composing atonal music which was abstract, highly structured, and extremely concentrated and brief. Webern felt that each individual note of a piece was important, and he used notes sparingly (music which uses brevity and is extremely concentrated is often called aphoristic, and the term aphoristic is often applied to Webern's music). In the 1920s, Webern began composing in the twelve-tone technique (later known as serialism) pioneered by Schoenberg.

During his lifetime, Webern did not achieve much success as a composer because his music was considered too abstract and atonal by the general public. He was forced to support his family through other means such as various conducting positions and teaching. During the 1950s and 1960s, other composers became interested in Webern's compositional style, particularly in features such as his use of brevity and the value of individual notes; his unique interpretation of serialism; and his innovative use of texture, rhythm and dynamics. Webern's musical works included vocal music such as songs, cantatas, a choral work, piano music and chamber music. The instrumentation Webern used was often unconventional such as his *Quartet Op. 22* which called for clarinet, saxophone, violin and piano.[15]

TECHNIQUE TIPS: *Opus 7* was composed by Anton Webern in 1910, and is entitled *Four Pieces for Violin and Piano*. Webern used an aphoristic style of composition in this piece, and the music is highly condensed and brief. It is an atonal piece, and Webern utilized an unusual palette of sounds and timbres using various instrumental effects. The selection used for this arrangement is taken from Webern's *Op. 7, Piece No. 1*, entitled "Sehr langsam." Webern's score indicates it should be played very slowly (*sehr langsam*, in German means "very slowly"), with a mute (*mit dämpfer* in German). Mutes are small clamps of wood, metal, rubber, leather or plastic, which fit onto the bridge and produce a softer, muted sound with a veiled quality.

This piece begins with a fingered harmonic:

Fingered harmonic

Harmonics are overtones of the string and produce soft, flutelike sounds when the string is lightly touched at specific fractional divisions (nodal points). Natural harmonics are produced on open strings, and artificial, stopped or fingered harmonics are produced on stopped strings. Artificial or fingered harmonics are produced by firmly pressing the first finger down on a note two octaves below the desired pitch, and then lightly touching the fourth finger a perfect fourth above the notated pitch. This divides the string into fourths, and the resulting sound is two octaves above the stopped pitch (less commonly used, are artificial harmonics with the finger lightly touching the string a third or fifth above the stopped notes). Webern begins his piece with a fingered harmonic using the first and fourth fingers. To play the first note of the piece, press your first finger down firmly on the D string for the note Eb (a low 1st finger), then lightly touch your fourth finger on the D string for the note Ab (a low fourth finger). This should produce a harmonic two octaves above the stopped note, with a light, silvery sound.

Webern's musical directions also call for *col legno* beginning in measure 5. *Col legno* is a term which means the bow should strike the string with the bow stick instead of the bow hair. To do this, turn your bow upside down so the wood of the bow stick is facing the strings, and gently let the stick of your bow bounce on the strings. This should produce a brittle, dry sound. As a side note, some professional string players do not like using their expensive bows to produce this sound, and use inexpensive bows when this effect is called for in extended passages in orchestral music. The piece ends with *pizzicato* (often abbreviated as *pizz.*), meaning the string should be plucked with the finger instead of being bowed.

SECTION 5.6

PIECE: SIMPLE GIFTS

Simple Gifts is a Shaker[16] dancing song, and is generally thought to have been composed in 1848 by Shaker Elder Joseph Brackett Jr. of the Maine Ministry.[17] It appears in many early manuscript collections of Shaker music, and one manuscript notes it was "composed by the Alfred Ministry June 28, 1848."[18] This melody became well-known and was elevated to the level of art music when it was used by composers in other compositions such as Aaron Copland's use of *Simple Gifts* in his 1944 ballet *Appalachian Spring* (Copland subsequently arranged his *Appalachian Spring* as an orchestral suite, and the *Simple Gifts* melody is prominently featured in this suite). Other notable uses of the *Simple Gifts* tune include Sydney Carter's 1963 *Lord of the Dance* music. *Simple Gifts* has one verse, and the lyrics are included below.[19]

Simple Gifts Text

'Tis the gift to be simple, 'tis the gift to be free,
'Tis the gift to come down where we ought to be,
And when we find ourselves in the place just right,
'Twill be in the valley of love and delight.
When true simplicity is gain'd,
To bow and to bend we shan't be asham'd,
To turn, turn will be our delight,
'Till by turning, turning we come round right.

TECHNIQUE TIPS: *Simple Gifts* was used for dancing, and the text accompanying the music emphasizes the dance nature of the piece with the words "turn, turn." It was called a quick dance by the Shakers, and should be played with a moderately fast tempo. As you play this simple dancing tune, try to maintain the momentum of the rhythm and melody with light and energetic bowing and slurs when needed.[20]

SECTION 5.7

PIECE: "BRAUL" FROM ROMANIAN FOLK DANCES

Fig. 5.4 *Bartók*

Béla Bartók (1881-1945) was a Hungarian composer, pianist, teacher and ethnomusicologist (ethnomusicology is the study of music in its cultural context, particularly music not affiliated with European art music). He began taking piano lessons from his mother at a young age, and began writing piano music when he was 9 years old. Bartók studied music at the Budapest Academy of Music, and in the early 1900s, he became interested in Hungary's nationalistic movement to create a specifically Hungarian style of music.

Bartók's initial research into what was then regarded as Hungarian folk music, found that much of this music was of recent origin by popular composers, and were artistic imitations of Hungarian peasant music. In collaboration with the musician Zoltán Kodály (1882-1967), Bartók began to collect and systematically study previously unknown Hungarian peasant songs. Many of their collections of folksongs were published (*e.g. A magyar néodak* published in 1924, which presented 8000 Hungarian folksong melodies collected and classified by Bartók and Kodály). Later, Bartók expanded his research efforts to Romanian and Slovakian folk music, and he eventually collected, recorded, transcribed and analyzed folk music in areas such as North Africa (Arabic music in Biskra, Algeria), Croatia, Turkey, and Bulgaria.[21] [22]

Bartók spoke of the impact his studies of folk music had on his compositions:

> The outcome of these studies was of decisive influence upon my work, because it freed me from the tyrannical rule of the major and minor keys. The great part of the collected treasure, and the more valuable part, was in old ecclesiastical or old Greek modes, or based on more primitive (pentatonic) scales, and the melodies were full of most free and varied rhythmic phrases and changes of tempi, played both *rubato* and *giusto*. It became clear to me that the old modes, which had been forgotten in our music, had lost nothing of their vigour. Their new employment made new rhythmic combinations possible. This new way of using the diatonic scale brought freedom from the rigid use of the major and minor keys, and eventually led to a new conception of the chromatic scale, every tone of which came to be considered of equal value and could be used freely and independently.[23]

Bartók used folk materials in many of his compositions, and took different approaches in his treatment of folk music. At times, he featured the folk melody as a rare jewel, and composed a simple arrangement to feature and highlight the melody. At other times, he did not quote folktunes directly, instead he imbued his compositions with folk music characteristics such as an expanded harmonic language and rhythm, with melodies that were either imitative or alluded to a folk music style. In many of his compositions, Bartók elevated folk music to the level of art music. His compositions included works in genres such as piano music, chamber music, orchestral compositions, theater music, an opera, ballets, choral music, songs, and folksong arrangements.[24] [25]

Bartok composed *Romanian Folk Dances* (*Román nepi táncok*) in 1915 for piano, and this composition is an example of Bartok adding a harmonized accompaniment to preexisting melodies. Bartok later arranged these dances for violin and piano, and for a chamber orchestra.

TECHNIQUE TIPS: The piece selected from Bartók's *Romanian Folk Dances* is the second dance, "Brâul." and this arrangement is based on Bartok's 1915 version for piano (*brâul* means "sash," and refers to a cloth belt worn by dancers). This is a dance piece, and the rhythm should be played freely, with *rubato* in many sections throughout the piece. *Rubato* means "robbed." It refers to a temporary robbing of time by either slowing or speeding the tempo or rhythmic value of notes in a passage of music. Although *rubato* is not indicated in the score of this arrangement, if you listen to recordings of this piece by orchestras or other musicians, it is likely that you will hear the use of *rubato* at the end of most of the musical phrases (*e.g.* measures 3-4; 7-8; 15-16; 19-20; 23-24; and 31-32). Other features of this arrangement include the use of dots over or under some of the notes, indicating a *spicatto* bow stroke should be used (*spicatto* is a bouncing, off-the-string stroke).

STUDY UNIT 6—NON-TRADITIONAL MUSIC

NON-TRADITIONAL MUSIC SECTIONS

Fig. 6.1 *Galaxy of Musicians*

SECTION 6.1

GYPSY MUSIC: THE BASSO

The Basso is a traditional piece of Gypsy music. The term Gypsy music is often used to refer to the music of the Roma. The Roma or Gypsies are thought to have migrated from northern India to Europe over 1,000 years ago, and their presence as entertainers and musicians in European royal musical courts beginning in the 1400s is well documented (the term Gypsy also refers to "Traveller" groups from other countries, but this brief description will focus on the Roma Gypsies). It should be noted that there is some controversy over using the term Gypsy. Some Roma regard Gypsy as a derogatory term, and prefer to be called by their tribal name or by the name Roma (Rom means man or person in the Gypsy language, Roma is plural, and Romani and Romanes are names for the Gypsy language).[1][2][3]

One of the reasons why it is difficult to characterize Gypsy music, is because the Roma musicians were both influenced by and exerted an influence upon the music of the countries they were living in. The following author described how this took place:

> Roma musicians absorbed music from the new territories, and in turn influenced the locals—you can hear it in everything from the modes and percussion of Turkey to the raw *duende* of Spanish flamenco. But their influence was greatest across the Balkans and Central Europe, where it was often the Romany musicians who earned their living by playing for village weddings, feasts and celebrations of all kinds. They became familiar with the music of different parts of the Balkans where they settled, adding their own flourishes, which in turn became standard fare for local musicians. The Roma would travel throughout the region, playing, taking in sounds and ideas and adding them to their own. It became commonplace to see Gypsy and Jewish klezmer musicians playing together, and klezmer took on some of the characteristics of Gypsy music and vice versa.[4]

Music scholar David Malvini attempted to define Gypsy music as being an emotive performance style containing the values of emotion, virtuosity and improvisation: "Roma musicians offered a different, 'Easternized' alternative to European performance practice. The positive trope of the exoticism became what I theorize as Gypsiness: the idea that improvisation combined with stunning virtuosity creates an emotionally charged atmosphere."[5]

TECHNIQUE TIPS: *The Basso* is a traditional Gypsy piece, and stringed instruments are often used to play the melody. This arrangement is in a minor key, and should be played with virtuosity, expressiveness and passion. If you find it too difficult to use separate, short bows when you play the rapid notes in measures 34-37 and 42-45, you could try using slurs for these sections. You may want to listen to different regional versions of *The Basso*, *e.g.* the Russian version sounds slightly different from Hungarian version, and each performance varies as musicians use improvisation and ornamentation to add their own unique style to the piece. To find different interpretations of *The Basso*, you could conduct an Internet search for different audio and video versions of *The Basso*, and pattern your playing after the style you like best.[6][7][8]

SECTION 6.2

KLEZMER MUSIC: ODESSA BULGARISH

Odessa Bulgarish is a traditional klezmer piece. The term klezmer is a Yiddish name that can either be applied to the type of music or the musician playing the music. It is derived from two Jewish words: *kle* (vessel or instrument) and *zemer* (song), literally meaning "instrument or vessel of song." Klezmer was first used to describe the traditional instrumental music of Yiddish speaking Jews in Eastern Europe. The roots of klezmer music stem from vocal styles of cantorial chanting, wordless melodies called *nigunim* (sung by Hasidic Jews), and local popular songs and dances. Klezmer music also reflects folk and cultural elements from the countries klezmer musicians lived in such as Russia, the Ukraine, Romania, and Poland (including the cross-influence of gypsy music—klezmer and gypsy musicians often played together and influenced each other's styles). When Eastern European immigrants began to emigrate to America in the 1880s, they brought their klezmer music traditions with them. Although there was a resurgence of interest in klezmer music in the 1920s in New York, it wasn't until the 1970s and 1980s that a revival of interest in klezmer music took place in the United States and then spread to other countries around the world.[9][10]

Instruments originally used in klezmer bands were a lead violin, second violin (or viola), bass or cello, and a cimbalom. A cimbalom is a hammered dulcimer, and klezmer musicians often used small, portable versions of the cimbalom (it is played with two wooden or metal mallets which are padded on the striking end). Flutes and a small drum were occasionally used, and beginning in the early 19th century, the clarinet became a prominent part of the klezmer band. In the late 19th and 20th centuries, additional instruments were added such as brass instruments, the accordion, bass guitar and percussion.[11]

Musicologists have noted similarities between klezmer and other improvisational styles such as gypsy music and jazz. Klezmer music originally began as an oral tradition (passed down from one musician to another orally, instead of through music notation), and although the basic harmonic and melodic structure of a piece may remain the same, the improvisatory capabilities of each musician often result in the interpretation and sound of the music varying each time a piece is played. Since klezmer music is based on cantorial singing from synagogues, many ornamental effects are used to try to imitate the sound of the human voice. For example, *krekhts* (Yiddish for moan), means the instrumentalist should try to create a wailing sound; *kneytsch* refers to imitating the sound of a sob or catch; and *tshok* refers to a laugh-like sound.[12] Additional characteristics of klezmer music include ornamentation such as trills, mordents (meaning alternate between the written note, one note above, then back to the written note), and vibrato. In klezmer music, vibrato is regarded as an ornament, and should be used selectively. When vibrato is used as a form of ornamentation in klezmer music, a fast, tight vibrato is used to ornament specific notes or sections.[13]

Klezmer music frequently uses minor keys and exotic sounding scales such as the klezmer *Ahava Rabboh* or *freygish* scale with its augmented second between the 2nd and 3rd degree of the scale. Augmented means raised, and when the term augmented is combined with a specific interval between notes, it means to raise the interval by a half-step. For example, an augmented second is a half-step larger than the interval of a perfect second. Some klezmer musicians assert that the Western system of scales does not adequately represent klezmer music, and point to a specific system of prayer modes used in synagogues as the basis for klezmer music. The names of these modes are derived from the sung prayers in which they are used, and the modes affect more than the scale used in the piece. Each mode represents a mood, and implies a certain way in which the notes in the scale should be used. Using the Western system of scales, the piece *Odessa Bulgarish* seems to be in the following harmonic minor key beginning on the note D.

Harmonic minor scale used in Odessa Bulgarish

Some Klezmer musicians assert that the tonality of *Odessa Bulgarish* is not based on the harmonic minor scale, but is instead based on a prayer mode used in klezmer music called *Mi Sheberach* ("He who blessed"). This prayer mode features an augmented fourth.

Mi Sheberach klezmer mode used in Odessa Bulgarish

When comparing the *Mi Sheberach* mode with the harmonic minor scale, the intervals between the notes are identical. Using the harmonic minor scale to analyze the piece, *Odessa Bulgarish* begins on the fourth degree of the harmonic minor scale, and when using the *Mi Sheberach* prayer mode, the piece begins on the first note of the *Mi Sheberach* mode. Although the differences between these two scales may seem insignificant, as mentioned above, klezmer purists assert that since prayer modes are used to shape the mood and affect the structure of klezmer music, the most accurate way to analyze and understand klezmer music such as Odessa Bulgur, is through the use of the appropriate prayer mode, the *Mi Sheberach* mode.[14]

TECHNIQUE TIPS: *Odessa Bulgarish* is a traditional klezmer piece originating in the Ukraine. Bulgarish refers to a popular klezmer dance form, and some music scholars have asserted that the bulgarish originated in Bessarabia as the *bulgareasca* (Bessarabia was later known as Moldavia and Moldova), and then spread as the klezmer bulgarish to the Eastern Ukraine (the name was later shortened to bulgar in America).[15] As noted above, this piece uses the klezmer mode *Mi Sheberach* with an augmented fourth. The bulgarish is a lively dance, and generally begins with an up-beat of three notes. Play this piece using an energetic dance tempo, and experiment with adding ornamental flourishes. You also may want to listen to different recordings or view video clips of *Odessa Bulgarish* and try to imitate some of the ornamentation and improvisational techniques that other musicians use in performing this lively klezmer piece.

SECTION 6.3

GREEK FOLK MUSIC: VARYS HASAPIKOS

Varys Hasapikos is a traditional Greek folk dance with a recognizable melody. Many aspects of Greek folk music are related to classical Greek and Byzantine church music, and the geographical location of Greece contributed to its folk music being influenced by many other nations. Dance has always played a prominent role in the lives of Greeks, and dance music comprises the largest category of Greek folk music.[16]

Western stringed instruments such as the violin have been used to perform Greek folk music for over 400 years. Small ensembles are often used to accompany dancing and singing, and the instruments in these ensembles often include the clarinet, violin, lute or guitar, *santouri* (hammered dulcimer), and occasionally a small drum and tambourine. Other frequently used Greek folk instruments include the plucked *laouto* or *bouzouki,*[17][18] and the *lyra*, a three-stringed bowed fiddle played with the body of the instrument resting on the player's knee. The *lyra* is sometimes used in place of the violin, particularly in locations such as the islands of Crete and Karpathos.

In the 1950s, a resurgence of interest in Greek folk music led to a renewed interest in the *lyra*. Tullia Magrini, a music scholar researching the history of a family of violinists from the Greek island of Crete, noted that the violin appears to have been brought to Crete at some point during the Venetian occupation from 1218-1682. Since instruments in the violin family were not invented until 1495-1505 in Ferrara, Italy, this could not have taken place until the 1500s or later. Although it is likely that other instruments from the violin family such as the cello and viola were also introduced to Greece at this time, these instruments apparently did not gain the popular status that the violin did in playing Greek folk music. It is interesting to note that despite the early arrival of the violin in the repertory and performance of Greek folk music, some Greek folklorist purists claimed the violin was an inappropriate instrument to perform traditional Greek folk music. Magrini asserted:

> Since 1955, in Greece, to perform Cretan music with violin was forbidden in all state mass media, because of the nationalistic policy and purism adopted by Greek folklorists. The violin, imported to Crete from Italy during the Venice domination, was interpreted as a foreign instrument, basically unrelated to the Cretan musical tradition, and banned, while the *lyra* was chosen as the heir and symbol of uncontaminated musical folklore.[19]

82

Magrini noted that attempting to exclude the violin from Greece was absurd, particularly in light of the violin's contributions towards Greek folk music:

> It must be stressed that the action of remodelling the musical history of Crete begun in the 1950s underrated the very important role that the violin and violin-players had had in working out an important repertoire of Cretan dances and fostered the artificial revival of the *lyra* that took place after 1955. When Naftis came back to Crete in 1976, the *lyra* had become the musical symbol of Cretan ethnic identity, even if its organological aspects, performance practice, and repertory gave evidence of the strong influence exerted on it by the violin tradition (According to the [Crete violinist] Papadakis, many *lyra* players started as violin players).[20]

Although Greek folklorists may regard the violin with distrust, hostility towards the violin is apparently not universally embraced in Greece, because the violin continues to play a prominent role in the performance of Greek folk music throughout Greece today.[21] [22]

TECHNIQUE TIPS: The *hasapikos* dance originated in Constantinople during the Byzantine period, and originally was the dance of the Butcher's Guild of Constantinople (Constantinople, now İstanbul, Turkey, was once part of the Greek empire, and in 1453, became part of the Ottoman Empire). Since this dance was popular throughout Greece, it is known as a Panhellenic dance. Panhellenic means of or relating to all the Greek people, and when a dance is called a Panhellenic dance, it means the particular dance is so well-known throughout Greece that it is not assigned to a specific region.

The *hasapikos* is generally performed as a male line dance, with a hand to shoulder hold. There are numerous variations of this dance. One variation of the *hasapikos* dance, the *syrtaki*, became popular when it was a featured dance in the movie "Zorba the Greek" (this movie was released in 1964, and "Zorba's dance" using the dance steps of a *syrtaki*, was performed to a piece composed by a contemporary Greek composer, Mikis Theodorakis). As a note of explanation, the *syrtaki* is a combination of two traditional dances: the *hasapiko*, danced in a slow tempo, and the *hasaposerviko*, a subgroup of the *hasapiko* and danced twice as fast. The *hasapiko* featured in this arrangement is called *Varys Hasapikos* (varys means heavy or slow, and *hasapikos* comes from the Greek word *hasapis* and means butcher). The tempo of this arrangement is *andante*, meaning a moderately slow, walking speed. As you play this music, imitate the deliberate walking tempo dancers might use to perform this traditional dance.[23] [24] [25] [26]

MEXICAN FOLK MUSIC: EL JARABE TAPATIO

El Jarabe Tapatio is a popular mariachi folk dance, with a very well known melody. Mariachi music is a form of Mexican folk music which originated in western Mexico, and became popular throughout all of Mexico as a symbol of Mexican nationalism and identity. Although the precise date when mariachi music began in Mexico is not known, stringed instruments used in mariachi music such as the violin, *vihuela* (a small, guitar-like instrument with 5 strings and a rounded back) and harp, were introduced to Mexico during the Spanish colonial rule of Mexico (1521-1821). Although the word mariachi is sometimes erroneously attributed to a derivation of the French word for marriage, scholars have determined that some of the first known uses of the word mariachi in Mexico came from letters and diaries written by Catholic priests in the 1850s. Here's an excerpt from a Catholic priest's 1859 diary entry describing mariachi music: "The musics, or as they say around there *mariache,* comprised of large harps, violins, and a bass drum, played incessantly."[27]

The term mariachi is used to describe the music, the dances performed to it, and the ensembles used to perform mariachi music. Traditional mariachi ensembles were comprised of string instruments such as violins, guitar-like instruments such as the *vihuela*, the *guitarrón* (a large 4-5 string bass guitar which later evolved into a 6-string guitar), and in some regions, the *guitarra de golpe* (a small five-string guitar). Some early mariachi groups also included a diatonic harp. Modern mariachi groups generally include trumpets along with violins, *vihuelas, guitarróns*, and acoustic guitars.

Mariachi music was originally considered a rural form of folk music for the "common" people (such as *mestizos*—racially mixed persons with Spanish and Native American ancestry). Mariachi music is based on many forms of *mestizo* folk music such as *son* (meaning song; plural, *sones*), *corrido, cancion, huapango* and *jarabe*. The musical form of *jarabe* is a type of *son* intended for dancing, and it emerged around 1800. During the time of Mexican independence from Spain and the decline of ecclesiastical influence, secular music in Mexico became more popular. *Sones* and *jarabes* became symbols of political insurgence and national identity, and *jarabes* gradually evolved into combinations of excerpts from *sones* and other popular melodies. After the Mexican Revolution in 1910, mariachi music was hailed as a symbol of nationalism, and soon became a popular form of music throughout Mexico.[28] [29] [30] [31] [32]

El Jarabe Tapatio is one of the most popular dances from Mexico as explained in the following quote:

> In the post-revolutionary era, numerous governmental efforts have promoted a common canon of folklore throughout the country…There is no greater archetype of this canon than "*El Jarabe Tapatío*."…Some of these *jarabes*, such as "*El Jarabe Tapatío*," were arranged for piano and published, becoming established as standard versions. In performances of "*El*

Jarabe Tapatío" in Mexico City in 1918, the Russian ballerina Anna Pavlova popularized choreographic innovations that further standardized the piece. By 1921, when, in Mexico City, performers premiered the version of "*El Jarabe Tapatío*" to be taught in the nation's public schools, its primacy and the title of "*El Jarabe National*" were fixed, though at the expense of losing much of its dynamic quality as a social dance.[33]

There is some debate regarding when *El Jarabe Tapatío* was first compiled. Some attribute it to a professor of music in Guadalajara, Jesús González Rubio (d. 1874), who purportedly compiled numerous *jarabes*, including an arrangement he made of *Jarabe Tapatio*.[34][35] Other sources attribute *El Jarabe Tapatío* to F. A. Partichela, who published a 1919 version in Mexico. One music researcher determined that the earliest printed version of *El Jarabe Tapatío* was a 1916 version arranged by A. Macias C., and this 1916 version was published in Texas.[36] There may be other earlier versions too, for example, another arrangement was written by the Mexican composer Manuel Maria Ponce. Ponce used the "Mexican folk tune" *Jarabe tapatio* as thematic material in a piece he composed in 1913 called *Rapsodia Mexicana II*. It was published by the Mexico City publisher A. Wagner y Levien, the same publisher who published F. A. Partichela's 1919 arrangement of *Jarabe tapatio*. Although all of these different versions and claims regarding the first publication date of *El Jarabe Tapatío* may be interesting, pinpointing an actual publication date may not really matter because most musicians consider *El Jarabe Tapatío* to be traditional Mexican folk music since it is a medley of popular songs such as:

- *Jarabe de Jalisco* – a *jarabe* from the state of Jalisco
- *Jarabe del Atole* – a well-known traditional *jarabe* from the late 1800's
- *Son del Palomo* – one of Mexico's most well-known *sones*
- a *Jarana Yucateca* – a popular dance style from the Yucatán Peninsula
- *Jarabe Moreliano* – a *jarabe* from the state of Michoacán
- *La Diana* – the final section of most *jarabes* [37]

The name *Jarabe Tapatio* is derived from different sources. Although *jarabe* does refer to a song (*son*) in the musical form of a dance, the word *jarabe* also means "syrup" in Mexican Spanish. Some scholars have also linked the word *jarabe* to the Arabic word *xarab* which means mixture of herbs, and there is some debate whether *jarabe* refers to the sweet courtship between the couples during the dance, or is a reference to the mixture of popular local songs used in creating this dance. The word *tapatio* refers to the region the *tapatio* dance came from (the Jalisco region), and the *tapatio* dance is a Mexican couples dance, in which the man dances the Spanish *zapateado* steps (a flamenco dance with syncopated heel and toe stamping in imitation of castanets). *Jarabe Tapatio*, a courtship dance, is nicknamed the Mexican hat dance, because during the dance, the man throws his hat at the feet of the woman. After she puts it on, they dance together.[38][39][40][41]

TECHNIQUE TIPS: As you play *Jarabe Tapatio's* famous compilation of Mexican folk songs and dances, maintain a lively dance tempo throughout the piece. This arrangement begins with a 6/8 meter with a strong triple pulse in each measure (ONE-two-three, FOUR-five-six). Beginning in measure 25, the meter changes to 2/4 with a strong two-beat pulse.

SECTION 6.5

CHINESE FOLK MUSIC

China encompasses a vast territory: approximately 3.7 million square miles. Although there are many ethnic groups in China (at least 55 minority nationalities), approximately 94% of the nation's estimated 1.3 billion population are Han Chinese. For this reason, when music scholars refer to Chinese music, it is often the music of the Han Chinese that they are referring to. Even within the Han Chinese, there are many cultural differences due to factors such as geography, historical events, and different dialects. The Chinese term *weidao* (meaning "flavor") describes these distinctions between regional styles and musical customs, and refers to a performer who sings or plays well in the "flavor" of a regional style.[42] [43] [44]

China has a rich heritage of art music and folk music traditions. Some scholars of Chinese music have divided the music into the following genres: court music, religious and ritual music, music of the literati, and folk (*minjian*) music. As a broad category, folk music is used to describe songs associated with work and physical labor, and music for weddings, funerals, festivals and entertainment (including instrumental music, song and dance music, and theatrical music).[45] [46] It should be noted that some music scholars feel that many Chinese folk traditions are as highly developed as classical art music, and therefore could be described as "folk-classical" traditions.[47]

The music scholar Alan Thrasher referred to the influence the Chinese government has played in the development of Chinese music:

> Traditionally, music in general was viewed by Chinese scholar-officials as an extension of government theory, and was therefore assigned a very large role in promoting government-sanctioned ideologies. Conformity, social harmony, and respect were highly-stressed values in all aspects of traditional culture, and music and the arts were expected to reflect these qualities. In terms of melodic style the use of anhemitonic pentatonic modal structures (with minimal intervallic tensions), relatively even beat subdivisions (eight- and sixteenth-note rhythms), related (rather than contrasted) thematic material, and group-oriented heterophonic performance all reinforce this sense of social harmony. Collective expression of a community, rather than individual achievement over others, is the dominant social orientation in Chinese creativity.[48]

Some of the main elements of Han music theory include notes (*sheng*), temperament and pitch (*lü*), scale (*diao*), melody (*qiang*), meter and rhythm (*pai*), and modal structure (*diaoshi*). The term mode refers to notes arranged in a specific scale or pattern of intervals, and modes are often used to structure the melody or tonality of a piece. The modal or basic tonal system used in Chinese music is often described as having a pentatonic structure (pentatonic comes from the Greek word *pente*, meaning five, and is often used to describe music using a five-tone pentatonic scale). The Gong Mode is an example of a pentatonic mode used in Chinese music. The name of this mode, Gong, refers to both the name of the pitch and the pentatonic mode built upon it. It should be noted that all Chinese music is not built upon the same pentatonic mode.

Gong Mode

Although a large portion of Chinese music, including folk songs, are based upon pentatonic modes, more than one version of a five-tone pentatonic scale is used, and other scales are sometimes used (*e.g.* seven-tone scales, and occasionally four, six and eight-tone scales). Melodies are often embellished with ornamentation and variations, and the concept of *jia hua* (meaning "add flowers") describes this concept of embellishment.[49] [50]

Rhythm in Chinese music is often described in terms of strong and weak beats (respectively, *ban* and *yan*). These beats are typically combined in groups of two or four beats (comparable to the Western concept of duple meter in 2/4 or 4/4). Triple and compound meters are not commonly used. Some of the techniques used to create form in Chinese music include repetition, elaboration and extended forms. One of the most common ways to create extended form in Chinese music is a suite (called *paitao*), where melodies are added one after another to create a long composition.[51]

Hundreds of folk instruments are used in China, and some of these are categorized as bowed lutes: stringed instruments, played with a bow. In China, a two-stringed bowed instrument called the *erhu* is sometimes called the "Chinese violin," "southern fiddle," or "spike fiddle." Chinese scholars have different theories for the *erhu*'s origin, and early versions of the *erhu* (such as the *huqin*), have been documented in China as far back as the Tang Dynasty (A.D. 618-907). The *erhu* is a popular folk instrument in China today, and as the illustration in figure 6.2 shows, it is made of wooden soundbox with a long wooden neck (the front of the soundbox is usually covered with snakeskin). Two metal strings extend from the bottom of the instrument to the top of the neck, and the pitch of the strings can be adjusted with tuning pegs. The two strings are generally tuned to the notes D and A (comparable to the open D and A used by the Western violin).

Fig. 6.2 *Erhu*

The *erhu* bow is generally made of bamboo wood, and the bow hair is usually made of horse hair. It is held upright to play (vertically), and the bow is pulled across the strings to produce a sound. The *erhu* is used to accompany singers or is part of folk ensembles (such as the Silk and Bamboo, *Jiangnan Sizhu* chamber ensemble), and in more recent years, the *erhu* has been used as a solo instrument.[52] [53]

Some *erhu* performers have adopted western violin performance techniques. Musicians such Liu Tianhua (1895-1932), a trained western violinist, introduced new *erhu* fingering, shifting and bowing techniques, and helped extend the conventional range of the *erhu* to three octaves (traditionally, the *erhu's* pitch range was one-and-a-half octaves). Western instrumental techniques such as vibrato, glissando, appoggiaturas and shifting are now commonly used by *erhu* performers, and modern professional *erhu* players have reached a high level of virtuosity on their instrument (today, the *erhu* is used to perform both Chinese art music and folk music).[54] [55] [56]

SECTION 6.6

PIECE: JASMINE FLOWER

Jasmine Flower is a popular Chinese folksong, and is frequently played by *erhu* players. There are two versions of this folk song, one from the Jiangsu province, and the other from the Zhejiang province, and their melodies and lyrics are different. Although this arrangement of Jasmine Flower is based on the Zhejiang province version, it is interesting to note that the Italian opera composer Giacomo Puccini (1858-1924) used the Jiangsu version of Jasmine Flower in his opera *Turandot* (Puccini used it as a unifying motif throughout *Turandot*. The Jiangsu version was also used during the 2008 Beijing Olympics as the theme song for medal ceremonies).[57] [58]

TECHNIQUE TIPS: Notice how the melody of *Jasmine Flower* uses only 5 notes: G,A,B,D,E. This is an example of the melody being structured around a pentatonic scale. Use smooth, flowing bows to play this delicate and lyrical melody. A few embellishments have been added to the music (grace notes), and you may want to experiment with adding more ornaments in the spirit of "jia hua" (meaning "add flowers").

SECTION 6.7

INDIAN CARNATIC MUSIC: SARA SARA

Sara Sara, a Carnatic instrumental piece, was composed by Tyāgarāja (1767-1847), a South Indian composer. Indian music is a highly developed art form, and although performing traditions have been transmitted orally, the theoretical basis for Indian music has been described in manuscripts for centuries. Two of the earliest manuscripts to describe significant aspects of Indian classical music theory are the *Nātyaśāstra* (musical portions in this manuscript are estimated to have been written in the 4th-5th centuries), and the *Sangīta-ratnākara* (written between 1210 and 1247).

There are two major musical systems in India: Carnatic (Karnatik), the music of southern India, and Hindustani, the music of northern India. Although the music of northern and southern India share many similarities, their music began to diverge from the thirteenth century on when northern India became subject to Islamic rule. Carnatic and Hindustani music are both based on two main elements: *raga* and *tala*. *Raga* is the basis for the melody, and is a specific set of notes in ascending and descending scales (melodic modes), and *tala* is the rhythmic pattern used in the music (metric cycles). In Carnatic music, *ragas* are classified into approximately 72 main scales or *melakartas*, and 35 principal rhythms or *talas*.

Carnatic music generally has three layers of musical activity:

1) **The melodic layer.** This layer is comprised of a melodic soloist, and melodic accompanist. Although the voice is often used for the melody, other melodic instruments frequently used include the violin, *vina* (a large plucked lute), *bansuri* (a bamboo flute), *nagasvaram* (an oboe), and saxophone.

2) **A percussion layer.** The most frequently used percussion instrument is a double-headed drum called the *mridangam*. Other percussion instruments include the *tavil* (a drum), a tambourine (*kanjira*), mouth harp (*morsang*) and a clay pot (the *ghatam*).

3) **The drone or *sruti* layer.** The *sruti* layer is often played by a specialized instrument such as the *tambura*, a four-stringed plucked instrument with a buzzing timbre.[59] [60] [61]

Ornaments or *gamaka* are another significant element of Carnatic music. There are three broad classes of ornamentation (*gamakas*) in Carnatic music: slides (ascending and descending), deflections (often performed as a rolling or sliding oscillation or shake of the note), and fingered stresses (often performed as a mordent, turn or grace note).[62] [63]

Three sample ornaments are presented below using western musical notation. The ornament's notation and ornament symbol are found in the first measure of each example, and the notation of what the ornament should sound like is found in the second measure of each example.

To play the ascending slide in Ex.1, use a sliding glissando or portamento sound as you let your finger slide from the F# up towards the note A.

Ex. 1 *Ascending Slide (etrajaru)*

To play the deflection in Ex. 2, using the tip of your finger, start on the note and roll back then forward twice as if you were doing two vibrato shakes in a backwards motion.

Ex. 2 Deflection (kampita)

To play the fingered stress in Ex. 3, let your finger rapidly strike the lower note in a fashion similar to playing a mordent. Since stringed instruments such as the violin, viola and cello are unfretted,

Ex. 3 Fingered Stress (pratyahata)

they are ideally suited to play the ornaments commonly used in Carnatic music. Balaswami Dishitar (1786-1858), younger brother of the composer Muttusvāmi Dīkshitar, was one of the earliest Carnatic musicians to adapt the violin to South Indian music,[64] and other early Carnatic violinists included Varahappa Iyer, Shri Vadivelu and Krishnaswami Bhagavatar. Due to the influence of these musicians, the violin has become one of the most popular instruments used as a melodic accompaniment for Carnatic vocal music, and as a solo instrument.[65] Although there are some Carnatic musicians who play the viola or the cello, these instruments are not as commonly used as the violin to play Carnatic music.

Western notation and fixed pitches are not typically used in Carnatic music. As a simplified explanation, Carnatic music uses the relative pitch of seven *svara*, or Carnatic scale degrees: *sa* (tonic or first degree of the scale); *ri* (or *re*, the second degree of the scale); *ga* (third); *ma* (fourth); *pa* (fifth); *da* (sixth); *ni* (seventh). These syllables, *sa-ri-ga-ma-pa-da-ni* are roughly comparable to the following *tonic solfa* notation used in English speaking countries: *do-re-mi-fa-sol-la-ti*. Other contributing factors to the ways Carnatic scales are structured include microtones, melodic elements and particular ways to treat scale degrees, but these complex topics will not be discussed at the present time. Since fixed pitches are not generally used with Carnatic music, Carnatic stringed instruments are often tuned differently than western stringed instruments. One of the common tunings for stringed instruments is: *sa-pa-sa-pa.* As an illustration of what this would sound like using western notation, if the vocalist or soloist decided the starting pitch of *sa* would be F (below middle C), Carnatic violin tuning for this piece would be:

Carnatic tuning   Western tuning

TECHNIQUE TIPS: *Sara Sara* was composed by Tyāgarāja (1767-1847), a famous South Indian composer who played a key role in the development of South Indian classical art music. He was one of the Carnatic "trinity" of composers (the other two members of the Carnatic trinity were Muttusvāmi Dīkshitar and Śyāma Śāstri). Tyāgarāja was noted for his use of devotion and emotion in his music, and most of his music was in honor of the Hindu god Rama. He composed over 700 pieces, and used many different *rāgas* in his compositions (most of his pieces were a song form called *kriti*, comprised of three parts called *pallavi*, *anupallavi* and *caranam*). Tyāgarāja's music is still regarded as a significant part of the repertoire of Carnatic music, and is frequently performed by

Carnatic musicians today. The raga (melodic mode) of *Sara Sara* is called *kuntalavarali* and the *tala* (meter) is *Adi* (the *Adi* meter or *tala* is grouped in an eight beats per measure pattern in this arrangement).[66]

Carnatic violinists and violists use a different playing position than western string players. Violinists and violists experimenting with Carnatic styles of playing may want to try this. Sit cross-legged on the floor, and let your scroll bend down and rest on the ankle of your right foot, and the bout of your violin or viola rest against your chest. Since your left hand won't need to hold the neck of your instrument up, it will be much easier to freely move your left hand up and down the fingerboard as you finger notes and perform improvised ornamentation (*gamaka*). You may want to experiment with ornaments such as slides, deflections and fingered stresses as you play this piece. If you'd like examples of how Carnatic stringed music really sounds, there are numerous online clips of Carnatic string players playing Carnatic music on the Internet (mostly violinists and a few violists). Visit a few of these sites, see how the music is performed, and experiment with imitating the sounds you hear. If you like this style of music, you may want to consider taking lessons from a Carnatic string player. Even today, Carnatic performing traditions are primarily transmitted orally from teacher (guru) to student (disciple or *shishya*).[67]

SECTION 6.8

ARABIC MUSIC: LONGA NAHAWAND

Longa Nahawand is a traditional Arabic musical piece, and this particular arrangement is based on a version composed by the Ottoman composer Tanburi Cemil Bey (1873-1916). Arab music is often defined as music traditions in the Arabic-speaking world, and it should be noted that there are many regional differences within this broad category. As a general overview, Arabic music originated in antiquity, and its present form today was shaped by factors such as:

1) **Contact with assimilated cultures.** Exposure to musical traditions of Syria, Mesopotamia, Byzantium, and Persia resulted in reciprocal influence and the cultivation of new forms of Arabic music.

2) **Contact with the Classical past.** The introduction of ancient Greek treatises to Islamic scholars resulted in many Arabic music treatises being written between the ninth and the thirteenth centuries.

3) **Contact with the Medieval West.** The Islamic occupation of Spain from 713-1492 brought contributions from Moorish Spain to Arabic musical forms.

4) **The influence of Turkish music.** Many elements of Arab music and Turkish music became assimilated during the Ottoman Empire's period of dominance over Arabic countries, particularly during 1517-1917.

5) **Contact with the modern West.** Beginning in the nineteenth and twentieth centuries, contact with the West resulted in the increased use of Western instruments, notation and theory.[68]

Classical Arab music is monophonic, and is based on melodic modes called *maqam* (plural, *maqamat*). These melodic modes often utilize microtonality: intervals that are smaller than the half-step and whole-step used in traditional Western art music. Unlike Western art music which uses twelve intervals to divide the octave, modern Arabic music theory divides the octave into twenty-four equivalent intervals (quarter-tones are used to achieve this scale). When Western notation is used to notate these quarter tones, a flat symbol with a slash through it is usually used for half-flats, and a sharp with only one vertical line is used for half-sharps. Some Arabic musicians use the 24 note scale as a point of reference, and assert some notes deviate even further from this scale by the slight interval of "a comma" (*kuma*). They use terminology such as the note should be played "a little high" or "a little low" to express how the note should be slightly lowered or raised from the note's standard position.[69] [70]

Arabic music frequently utilizes rhythmic patterns or metric modes called *'iqa*, played by percussion instruments. Each *'iqa* has a pattern of strong and weak beats which can range from two to twenty-four or more. It should be noted that some Arab music scholars assert that all Arabian music does not utilize rhythmic patterns, and that some genres utilize a free rhythmic-temporal organization.[71] [72] [73]

Improvisation is a key component of Arabic classical music. Arabic music employs various forms of improvisation such as forms that are entirely improvised, partially improvised forms and rhythms inserted in a composed piece, and improvised ornaments used within a composed piece. Some of the ornaments used in instrumental music include turns, trills, grace notes (above and below), glissando and vibrato. Although great freedom is used in these improvisations, established modal patterns are used to structure, develop and resolve these improvised forms. One of the most highly regarded forms of instrumental improvisation is called *taqsim* (plural, *taqasim*). The Arabic scholar and musician Ali Jihad Racy asserted that Arabic musical improvisation is not only used for affective reasons (on a stylistic and connotative level), but also for symbolic reasons (for social and artistic values). Racy described the effect improvisation in Arabic music can have on listeners:

> Instrumental and vocal improvisation, which may be heard in combination with non-improvised compositions or alone, are known to require extraordinary skill, talent, and inspiration, and to generate deeply felt emotions within the listeners. When properly performed they are considered ecstatically moving, as well as technically sophisticated.[74]

Some of the instruments commonly used today in Arab music include traditional Arabic instruments such as the *qānūn* (a plucked, boxed zither), *'ud* (a short-necked lute), and *nay* (reed flute), as well as Western European instruments such as the violin (during the 19th century, the European violin began to replace the Arabic spike fiddle or *kamanja* in most Arab countries). After World War I, ensembles of Arabic folk instruments called *takht* (meaning "perform") were expanded into an orchestra that included other members of the violin family.[75]

Although most Arab musicians hold the violin, viola and cello in the Western style of playing, members of the violin family are generally tuned differently. Here is an example of a common Arabic tuning for the violin (G D G D instead of the Western tuning for violins: G D A E).[76] [77] [78]

Violin Tuning

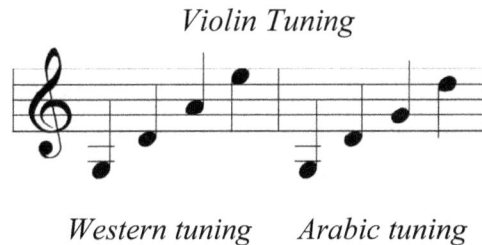

Western tuning   *Arabic tuning*

TECHNIQUE TIPS: The piece *Longa Nahawand* uses the Nahawand *maqam*. This *maqam* is similar to the Western harmonic minor scale as it ascends, and the Western natural minor scale as it descends.

Nahwand maqam

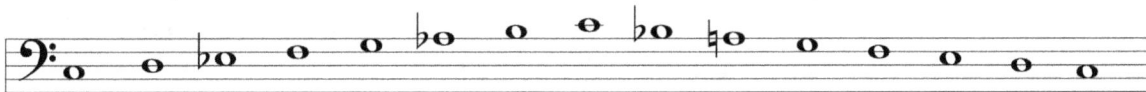

Longa is a traditional form of music used in Arabic and Middle Eastern music. It is a fast dance form that originated in Turkey or Eastern Europe.[79] Although there are many versions of *Longa Nahawand* (different musicians often use their improvisatory skills to create their own interpretation of *Longa Nahawand*), this arrangement is based on a version of *Longa Nahawand* composed by the highly regarded Ottoman Empire composer Tanburi Cemil Bey (Tambouri Djemil Bey). Bey was born in Istanbul in 1873 and died of tuberculosis at the age of 43 in 1916. He was a prominent composer of instrumental art music during the late period of the Ottoman Empire. Bey was a skilled performer on many instruments, including the violin, as well as Turkish instruments such as the *kemençe* (a small, three-stringed bowed fiddle played with the instrument placed upright and resting on the performer's knee). Bey also played a Turkish instrument called the *tanbur* (a long-necked, plucked lute), and a bowed version of the *tanbur* called the *yayli tanbu*. Bey was renowned for his *taksim* (instrumental improvisations on melodic modes called *maqam*, or *makam* in Turkish), and some of his early recordings on records have been digitally re-mastered and can still be heard today.[80] [81] [82] [83] [84]

As you play this arrangement of *Longa Nahawand,* use a lively dance tempo. You may want to try adding a few ornamental embellishments such as turns, trills, grace notes, slides and glissandos. In Arabic instrumental music, vibrato is also considered an ornament, and is often played by using light pressure to rapidly play the finger just above the intended note—the upper neighboring finger.

Arabic slides are short and fast, somewhat like a vocal sigh. To achieve the effect of an Arabic slide on your instrument, use the finger of the intended pitch as you slide. A few ornaments have been added to the score for you to try: slides in measures 11 and 12, and grace notes in the last two measures of the piece (measures 39-40).[85] [86]

SECTION 6.9

FIDDLE MUSIC OVERVIEW

Fiddle is a broad term, and is used to describe a stringed instrument, played with a bow (technically, a fiddle is categorized as a chordaphone). In colloquial language, fiddle is often used to describe a member of the violin family, the violin in particular. Throughout music history, the term fiddle has been applied to various instruments such as the medieval fiddle, Renaissance fiddle, and numerous folk instruments throughout the world. Some of the materials folk fiddles are made of include bamboo, gourd or wood, with bellies made of skin or wood, and one or more strings. Just a few of these varied types of folk fiddles include spike fiddles used in the Middle East such as the *rabāb* and *kamāncheh*; China's *huqin* and *erhu;* Mongolia's *huur;* and one-stringed fiddles used throughout West Africa (depending on the specific African country, numerous names are used for these African fiddles such as *kwakuma, ngime*, and *kuliktu*). The term fiddle is also used with folk instruments such as Norway's Hardanger fiddle.[87] [88] [89] [90] [91]

Fig. 6.3 *Fiddlin' Bill Hensley*

Fiddle music is another general term, and is used to describe a vast number of styles ranging from ethnic music played by folk fiddlers, to folk fiddle styles of playing. Although much of the information provided in this overview is directed towards the violin or fiddle, it should be noted that fiddle music is also played by other members of the violin family such as the viola and cello, and the information provided in this section can be applied to all members of the violin family. The following chart highlights some of the major folk fiddle styles of playing. It does not include ethnic music played by folk fiddles, and is by no means comprehensive. Many styles of fiddle playing have regional variations and sub-categories of varied styles, and an entire course could be devoted to each style of fiddle playing (each, with its own interesting origin and unique style of playing).[92] [93] [94] [95]

FIDDLE STYLES CHART

AMERICAN FIDDLING [96-109]

	Bluegrass	Bluegrass music is a style of country music that became popular in the 1940s, largely due to the music of Bill Monroe and his group the Blue Grass boys. Monroe and his country music band used distinctive vocal harmonies along with traditional acoustic instruments such as the fiddle, mandolin, banjo, guitar and bass. Bluegrass music incorporated Appalachian fiddle and vocal traditions with country, blues and gospel music, and the result was a unique style of music that is still popular today. The technique required to perform bluegrass music can be demanding, and virtuoso playing by instrumentalists is frequently utilized. The tempos are often extremely fast, and instrumentalists need to be prepared to "take a break" meaning, the instrumentalists take turns playing an improvised solo break while the other musicians provide a harmonic and rhythmic background. Fiddle players frequently use a lot of string crossings and shifting, including shifting while using double-stops. Bluegrass fiddlers often use double-stops with fingered chords to provide a harmony a third or sixth above or below the melody. Fiddle players also need to be prepared to employ slides with the left hand, incorporate blue notes into the music (a flatted third and seventh or fifth of the piece's scale), and utilize percussive, often syncopated bowing patterns such as the double shuffle used in the fiddle tune *Orange Blossom Special.*
	Cajun	Cajun music is a style of traditional folk music associated with Cajuns in southwestern Louisiana. Cajuns are descendants of Acadians, French colonists who settled in Acadia in the early 1600s (Acadia once included parts of the Canadian Maritime provinces such as Nova Scotia, New Brunswick, and Prince Edward Island, as well as parts of New England). In 1713, France ceded control of what is now Nova Scotia to the British, and in 1755, refusal by Acadians to swear loyalty to the British crown, resulted in the Great Expulsion. Between 1755 and 1763, 75% of Acadians were deported. Many Acadians settled in present-day southwest Louisiana where they became known as Cajuns (the term Cajun is a corruption of the word Acadian). Cajun music is a blending of its French roots with folk music from other

		countries and regions. It interacted with and absorbed features from Scottish and Irish music (from the Acadia period); new tunes for reels, hoedowns and square dances (from southern white folk music); syncopation, percussion idioms and improvisational singing and blues style (from black American music); terraced singing styles (from Amerindian music); a syncopated Carribean beat (from Saint-Domingue immigrants); and incorporated new instruments such as the accordion (from Germany), and the guitar (from Spain). Cajun music is often played by two fiddlers, one playing the melody, and the other playing a rhythmic accompaniment (often at a lower pitch). Some of the stylistic characteristics of Cajun fiddle music include a driving, rhythmic bowing, and bowing patterns such as the shuffle bow. Double stops are frequently used, including the effect of playing two strings together constantly (either with an open string as a drone effect, regular double stops, or by doubling the pitch an octave higher or lower). Ornaments include the use of blue notes, slides and trills.
	Old-time	Old-time fiddle music (sometimes called "old timey") is often defined as danceable old-time fiddle tunes (what one might have encountered at a late 19th century Saturday night dance in the rural Appalachian mountain region). Although old-time fiddle music is considered to be traditional American folk music, the repertory reflects its Anglo-Celtic roots (tunes and traditions from Scottish, English and Irish music). The interpretation of these tunes include aspects of black American music *(e.g.* phrasing, and syncopation). Dance forms used in old-time rural dance music include the American square dance (based on the French *contredanse*), the American hoedown (derived from the British hornpipe and reel), and polkas and waltzes (often modified version of social dances in duple and triple meter). Jigs, the two-step, rag, and *schottische* are a few of the other popular dances often associated with old-time fiddle music. Some of the stylistic characteristics of old-time music include the use of a simple, recognizable melody; double stops and drones; and basic bow strokes such as the shuffle and the double shuffle. Additional old-time techniques include foot-stomping and "beating straws." "Beating straws" requires an assistant to beat a rhythm with two

		broom straws on two open strings of the fiddle while the fiddler bows a melody on the opposite two strings (steel knitting needles or hardwood sticks are sometimes used for this "beating straws" effect). Some attribute the term "old-time" to a marketing ploy used in the 1920s to promote record sales of white, rural, agrarian Southerners in the Appalachian mountain region (although terms such as "hillbilly" were also used for these early recordings, some considered "hillbilly" to be a pejorative term). Although early recordings of country music in the 1920s and 1930s do appear to be where the term "old-time" was first used, a revival of interest in "old-time" music has led to multiple modern interpretations of its meaning. Old-time music is largely credited as being the original source for country music, and eventually led to many regional variations. Although country music originally featured fiddles in prominent roles, the use of fiddles in country music soon receded into an accompaniment role, and since country music largely is a vocal form today, it will not be included in this brief overview of fiddle styles.
	Western swing	Western swing is a form of popular music that originated in Texas during the 1930s. Western swing integrated country music with Mexican fiddle music, blues, and the big band or "swing" style of jazz. Additional characteristics of Western swing include the prominent use of fiddles, electrified instruments, and horns, winds and piano (these instruments were added to create a big band feel). The repertory of western swing is based on songs, and is an eclectic mix of country music, blues, jazz and popular music. Although the style is predominantly a vocal one, fiddles are prominently featured, and multiple fiddles are often used. In western swing music, fiddles are called on to use techniques such as improvisation (often an improvised version of the melodic line), riffs between sections (a riff is a short, repeated melodic pattern), and the use of a "swing" feel while playing music. Swing rhythm often refers to playing with a triplet feel such as interpreting eighth notes as follows: *Swing Rhythm*

	CANADIAN FIDDLING [110-114]	
	Anglo-Canadian	Found in English-speaking parts of Canada, Anglo-Canadian fiddle is a mixture of Scottish, Irish, English, German and United States fiddle styles and music.
	Cape Breton	Cape Breton, an island off of Canada's east coast, has a style of fiddling rooted in the Scottish Gaelic tradition (primarily the Highlands form of Scottish fiddle). This style of music is also referred to in Canada as "Cape Breton Scottish music" or "Scottish fiddling." Forms of Cape Breton music frequently played are reels, hornpipes, jigs and strathspeys.
	French-Canadian (*Québécois*)	French-Canadian fiddle music (also known as *Québécois* fiddle) is a fiddling style found in French speaking parts of Canada such as Quebec and Acadia. Although Acadia, once settled by French colonists in the 17th century is now part of the Canadian Maritime provinces, many Acadians retain strong ties to their original culture and identity (see Cajun music for more Acadian information). The French-Canadian style of fiddle music is a mixture of French folk music with Irish and Scottish fiddle styles. Characteristics include intricate and lively bowing, and the fiddler often adds percussive element such as the fiddler clogging with both feet while playing. Syncopation is frequently used, and the music often emphasizes the first beat of the measure. Predominant forms of fiddle music used in this style include the reel (in cut time), the march, and the *six-huit* (a tune in 6/8). Extra measures, beats or changes in meter are frequently added to suit the melody, and when this occurs, these irregularly structured pieces are called "crooked" tunes or *airs tordus*.
	Métis	The Métis people are descendents of European fur traders and Indian women living on the Plains in west central North America. Métis fiddle music can be found in Canada and parts of the northern United States (*i.e.* Canadian provinces such as Manitoba, Alberta and Saskatchewan; parts of Ontario, British Columbia and the Northwest Territories; and North Dakota and Montana in the United States). The Métis style of fiddle music is a unique blend of European styles such as French, Scottish and Irish reels, jigs and waltzes, with the dance forms and rhythms of Plains Indian music. Percussive accompaniments to the tunes are often supplied by heel tapping or

		spoons, and the music is often characterized by an uneven and irregular beat and meter that create a bounce in the music (short bowing patterns also contribute to this bounce). Asymmetric musical phrases are another characteristic, and a barless structure is generally used.
ENGLISH FIDDLING[115]		
		English fiddle music shares many tunes in common with its Scottish and Irish neighbors. Beginning in the mid-1600s, numerous collections of English dances were published such as John Playford's 1651 *English Dancing Master*. English dance tunes became widely used by fiddlers and dance masters throughout the British Isles (Playford's dancing music became popular in America too). Country dances such as the 17th-century English country dance included dances in a circle, square and longways formations, and these dances contributed to the development of the American square dance. Other popular forms of English fiddle music included jigs, hornpipes, airs, reels (based on Scottish music), Morris dances, and beginning in the 1800s, waltzes, polkas, *schottishes* and marches.
IRISH FIDDLING[116]		
	Clare	Clare fiddle music generally features slower tempos than the fiddle music from other Irish regions. This enables the player to focus on the melodic features of the music. Long, fluid bow-strokes, slurs, and extensive left-hand ornamentation are some of the characteristics of the Clare style of fiddle music. Ornaments frequently used include the left-handed roll (comparable to a turn in classical violin technique).
	Dongegal	Donegal fiddle music features a style that reflects the influence of Scottish fiddling. Donegal fiddle repertory includes Scottish music such as the Highland fling (also called *schottisches*) and *strathspeys* along with other traditional Irish tunes such as reels, jigs, hornpipes and airs. The tempo of Donegal fiddle music is generally fast, and single-note bowing with short strokes is emphasized. Instead of using extensive ornamentation with the left hand (as in other Irish fiddle styles), Dongegal fiddling uses the bow-hand to play ornaments such as trebling (this technique requires the player to play three notes using the same pitch in a triplet pattern with three short bow strokes).

	Dongegal *(cont.)*	Double stops and droning are additional characteristics of this style of fiddle playing, (these sounds are used to imitate the sound of the Scottish Highland pipes—bagpipes).
	Sliabh Luachra	Sliabh Luachra (The Mountain of Rushes), is a style of Irish fiddle music that is also called the Cork-Kerry style. The repertory features fast and lively dancing music, and this music is often used for set dances. Popular dances include polkas and slides (a dance tune in the form of a single jig), along with traditional Irish jigs and hornpipes. Slow airs are also commonly used in this regional style. Open strings are used to provide a drone, and when more than one fiddler is playing, the tune is often played an octave below (Donegal fiddle music uses this technique too). Ornamentation is achieved mainly with the left hand, and the bow hand provides the music with a characteristic rhythm and swing.
	Sligo	Sligo, an area in the far northwest of Ireland, has a fast and light fiddle style with a rhythm that some describe as having a pulsating lift, bounce and swing. Melodic lines are often highly ornamented with complex mixtures of short and long rolls, single and double grace notes, and trebles. Double stopping is frequently used, and both long and short bows are employed. Sligo fiddle players often use improvisation and variations as they interpret traditional tunes in their own unique style of playing.
SCANDINAVIAN FIDDLING [117-126]		
	Norway	Although the term Scandinavian fiddling is often used to describe fiddling in the Scandinavian region of Norway, Sweden, Denmark, Finland and Iceland, the fiddle music of Norway and Sweden are the most well-known fiddle styles in this region. *Slåtter,* a general term for traditional Norwegian folk music, is a frequently used form of Norwegian fiddle music. Specific *slåtter* dance forms include the *halling* (a solo man's dance with a fast, duple meter), *gangar* (a couples dance with a duple meter and a slow and steady pace), and *springar* (a couples dance in triple meter—*springar* is also called *pols* in Norwegian, and *polska* in Swedish music). Dance music introduced to Norway from other European countries is labeled *gammaldans,* and includes forms such as the polka, mazurka and waltz. The Norwegian fiddle tradition includes both the regular fiddle

	Norway (*cont.*)	(violin), and Norway's national instrument, the Hardanger fiddle (originally used in south central Norway). The Hardanger fiddle is similar to a violin, and has an additional four or five sympathetic strings below the fingerboard, and a nationalistic form of decoration (see Section 4.5 for an illustration of the Hardanger scroll). Fiddle techniques used in Norwegian fiddle music by both the Hardanger fiddle and violin include the frequent use of scordatura (tuning the instrument to notes other than the traditional G-D-A-E pitches), irregular or syncopated rhythms which are often produced by asymmetrical bowing patterns, and foot stomping.
	Sweden	Sweden shares many folk music traditions with Norway and other Scandinavian countries. *Spelmansböcker*, 18th-19th century Swedish fiddle tune books, share some of the same repertory with other Scandinavian countries. The music of Central and Western Europe also influenced Swedish folk music. Some of the music forms used in Swedish fiddling include popular dance tunes used throughout Scandanavia such as the *polska, waltz, schottische, polka* and *mazurka.* The *polska,* a dance in 3/4 time, is one of the most popular dances in Swedish folk music, and is derived from the European *polonaise.* Several forms of the *polska* are used, and it is generally played slower than a waltz, with a beat emphasis of ONE-two-THREE in each measure. Other common Swedish fiddle tunes include the *gånglåt* (a walking or marching tune), *brudmarsch* (a wedding march), and *skänklåt* (often played at weddings when gifts are given to the bride and groom). Some fiddle players embellish their music with double stops, triplets, and syncopation or rhythmic variations to the music. Scordatura is frequently used, and one of the most common re-tunings is A-D-A-E (this tuning is often used in the western parts of Sweden). Swedish fiddle music also uses the standard violin tuning G-D-A-E. Although the fiddle (violin) has always been the predominant instrument associated with Swedish folk music, Sweden also has a folk fiddle called the *nyckelharpa* (also called a keyed fiddle). Instead of using fingers to stop the strings, *nyckelharpas* have wooden keys that are pressed to stop the strings and create different pitches (these keys are attached to tangents under the string that reach up and press against the string to change the note's pitch). A short, curved bow is used to play the *nyckelharpa,* and like the Hardanger fiddle,

	Sweden (*cont.*)	the *nyckelharpa* has sympathetic strings under the fingerboard that resonate while the instrument is being played. Several versions of the *nyckelharpa* have been used throughout its history (the earliest picture of a *nyckelharpa* dates back to 1350). Since the 1970s, a revival of interest in Swedish folk music traditions has led to a resurgence of interest in the *nyckelharpa*. Four versions of the instrument are used today, and one of the most popular versions is a chromatic *nyckelharpa* developed in the 1920s. It has a three octave range, and has three melody strings, one drone string, 12 resonance strings, and approximately 37 wooden keys.
SCOTTISH FIDDLING[127]		
	Borders	Borders fiddle music often uses a heavy style of double stopping and chording (chording adds harmonic accompaniment to a piece, and is generally done using double stops). Popular forms of Borders fiddle music include hornpipes and airs. Fiddlers frequently play in pairs or trios, and the music is embellished with techniques such as slurs, bowing notes with single strokes, and snap bowing. Snap bowing is a technique where two notes are bowed in the same direction (often a dotted quarter followed by a sixteenth note), with a bite or *martelé* sound on the second note, and a slight space or rest between the notes. This is not the same thing as the Scotch snap, a Scottish rhythmic pattern used in *strathspey* music (see Fiddle Tunes Chart for an example of the Scotch snap and *strathspey*).
	East Coast	The East Coast style of fiddle music is more technically challenging than other regions of Scotland, and East Coast fiddle music is related to classical forms of music and traditional violin technique. Some of the music requires the fiddler to use higher positions (other regions predominantly use first position), and tunes often use difficult keys such as those with flats. Chromatic passages, double stops, triple stops and unison notes are frequently used, and bowing styles include staccato and the up driven bow (the up driven bow is a quick down bow followed by three consecutive up-bows). Ornaments include classical turns and trills, and musical forms include dances used throughout Scotland such as *strathspeys*, reels, jigs, marches and airs.

	Orkney	The Orkney fiddle style utilizes a simple, flowing bow stroke (slurs are not commonly used), a clear statement of the melody, and little or no vibrato. Other than occasional grace notes, ornaments are seldom used. Keys frequently used include A, D and G, and most of the music is in first position. Orkney fiddlers often hold their instrument angled down, and some of the main dance forms used in Orkney fiddle music are polkas and reels.
	Shetland	The Shetland fiddle style of playing was influenced by Norwegian music and the Hardanger fiddle. Double stops are easily played on the Hardanger fiddle (this is because its bridge is flatter than a violin's bridge), and Shetland music imitates this sound with a technique called "ringing strings" (open strings are played above or below the string the melody is played on). Double stops, playing in octaves and scordatura tuning are frequently used, and keys are often changed within a tune. Syncopated rhythms and strong accents are employed, often through the use of bowing techniques such as "back bowing" (this bowing uses an up bow on the strong beat of the bar, often producing an accent). Other bowing techniques include cross bowing (the first note of the slur begins on the off beat of this bowing pattern; *e.g.* a dotted eighth, followed by a sixteenth note slurred to a dotted eighth). Musical forms frequently found in Shetland music include: dance music such as reels and hornpipes; descriptive or listening pieces such as airs; ritual music such as wedding marches; and work music such as mill tunes (mill tunes were once played while mechanical work was being done in the mills).
	West Coast Highland	West Coast Highland fiddle music frequently imitates the sound of the bagpipe through the use of ornamentation and drones. When grace notes are used for ornaments, they often are played rapidly in imitation of bagpipe grace notes, and tunes frequently use only the notes of a bagpipe scale (tunes in major keys often flatten the seventh note, in imitation of the bagpipe scale). When more than one fiddler is present, tunes are frequently played in octaves. Bowing is generally done separately in the middle of the bow, and ornamentation includes triplets and birls (birls are a pattern of three identical pitches played with separate bows, often in the rhythm short-short-long). Popular forms of Highland dances include the Highland reel; marches (including the 2/4 pipe march, a form used by bagpipes); airs (often played with a free rhythm); *strathespeys*; and jigs.

FIDDLE TUNES

The following fiddle tunes chart provides information about selected fiddle music forms.

FIDDLE TUNES CHART [128-134]	
Air	A melody, tune or song. In fiddle music, airs generally are played slowly, often with *rubato*, and are not dance tunes.
Breakdown	A general term for fast, lively duple (2/4) and quadruple (4/4) dance tunes (the breakdown is synonymous with the hoedown).
Contredanse	Also referred to as *contra dance*, *contredanse* is French for "country dance," and this dance form was derived from the English country dance. The French called a set of *contredanses*, "*quadrille de contredanses*," and this was later shortened to *quadrille*. The square dance is considered to be based on the French *quadrille* or *contredanse*.
Crooked tunes	A French-Canadian form of fiddle music, crooked tunes are irregularly structured pieces with extra measures, beats or changes in the meter which have been added to suit the melody (also called *airs tordus*).
Gangar	A Norwegian couples dance with a duple meter and a slow and steady pace.
Halling	A Norwegian dance for a solo man in a fast, duple meter.
Hoedown	A general term for a fast, lively duple (2/4) or quadruple (4/4) dance tune (the hoedown is synonymous with the breakdown).
Hornpipe	A lively British dance, popular during the 16th-19th centuries. Meters used in the hornpipe dance were 2/4, 4/4, and 3/2 (3/2 was the meter used in the British country dance; a dance form similar to the reel, but with a different meter). The tempo of the hornpipe is generally slower than a reel, and rhythms most commonly encountered in hornpipe fiddle dances include 2/4 and 4/4 dotted rhythms such as: *Hornpipe Rhythm*

Jig	The jig, a popular and lively dance that originated in Ireland, is popular throughout the British Isles. There are three main forms of jigs: *Single Jig* *Double Jig* *Slip Jig*
March	A piece with a steady, walking (or marching) beat in duple meter (2/4 or 6/8). Marches are often used for events such as weddings and military processionals.
One step	A ballroom dance with quick, walking steps, performed to a fast march in 2/4 or 6/8 time (the one step later evolved into the quickstep and "trot" dances such as the foxtrot).
Polka	Originally a peasant round dance from Bohemia, the polka is a lively couples dance in duple meter (2/4). The typical rhythm is: *Polka Rhythm*
Polska	The polska is derived from the Polish dance *polonaise,* and it is a Scandinavian dance in 3/4 time (there are several forms used). The polska is generally played slower than a waltz, and the beat emphasis is ONE-two-THREE in each measure.
Quadrille	Quadrille was originally the name for a French dance, and it comes from the French expression for a set of *contredanses*, "quadrille de contredanses" (this was later shortened to quadrille). The square dance is considered to be based on the French quadrille or *contredanse*. Fiddle tunes called quadrilles often have meters of 6/8 (sometimes 2/4).
Quickstep	A fast version of the foxtrot. The quickstep uses a duple meter, and regular, four-bar phrases.

Rag	Rag is a piece composed in the musical style called ragtime, a style that features a ragged or syncopated rhythm. Rags are often in duple meter (2/4 or 4/4).
Reel	Originally a Scottish dance, the reel is a fast dance with duple (2/4) or quadruple (4/4) meter (typical Scottish meters are 2/2, 2/4, or 6/8). It generally has a binary form (two parts).
Riff	A short, repeated melodic pattern.
Schottische	The *schottishe* is similar to a slow version of a polka. It is a round dance, often in 2/4 time. Different variants of the *schottishe* include the Highland *Schottishe* (the Scottish Highland Fling) and the British Barn Schottish (the barn dance, which was a couples dance).
Slåtter	A general term for traditional Norwegian folk music. A few of the specific forms of slåtter include *halling*, *gangar* and *springar*.
Slide	The slide is basically a single jig, and is a dance form used in Ireland.
Springar	A Norwegian couples dance in triple meter. This dance is also called *pols* in Norwegian, and *polska* in Swedish music.
Square-dance	A popular early American dance, based on the *contredanse*. This dance is performed by sets of four couples facing each other in a square, and dance moves are announced by a caller.
Strathspey	A lively Scottish dance that features the Scotch Snap rhythm (also called Scots Snap) in both the regular and inverted form. The *strathspey* is usually in quadruple time, includes many dotted notes, and is a slower version of a reel. *Scots Snap Rhythm* *Strathspey Rhythm*

Swing	Swing rhythm often refers to a triplet feel such as interpreting eighth notes as follows:	$\lceil 3 \rceil$ ♫ = ♩♪ *Swing Rhythm*
Two step	A fast American ballroom dance, generally with a 6/8 meter. The rhythm in each bar is: quick-quick-slow.	
Waltz	A slow dance in triple meter, often with an accent on the first beat of the measure (*e.g.* ONE, two, three; ONE, two, three).	

SECTION 6.11

PIECE: AMERICAN FIDDLE MEDLEY

This American fiddle medley is a brief arrangement of three traditional, old-time fiddle pieces: *Bile Them Cabbage Down, Devil's Dream,* and the *Shuffle*. These pieces are commonly found in old-time American fiddle music collections. *Bile Them Cabbage Down* (also known as *Boil them Cabbage Down*), a reel, has been traced to an English country dance called *Smiling Polly* (a 1765 version is one of the earliest extant copies).[135] *Devil's Dream*, another reel, originated in Scotland, and an early version appeared in 1790 under the title: *The Devil Among the Taylors* (*The Devil Among the Taylors* or *Tailors* is still used as the title for this piece in the British Isles).[136] The final section called *Shuffle*, is a simplified version of the double shuffle, a bowing pattern frequently used in fiddle music. The shuffle uses the bowing pattern long-short-short, and is notated as follows:

Shuffle Bowing Pattern

The double shuffle is a 16-note bowing pattern, and uses two or more strings. Notice how in the example below, every third note uses a string crossing to reach to a different note in the following manner: d-d-A-d-d-A-d-d-A-d-d-A-d-d-A-d (the pattern is then repeated). This results in a syncopated feel to the rhythm (syncopation means to shift the musical accent from a strong beat to a weak one).

Double Shuffle Bowing Pattern

Double stops are frequently used in the shuffle bowing pattern, as in the following double shuffle excerpt from *Orange Blossom Special*.

Orange Blossom Special Double Shuffle Bowing

Double stops are commonly used in fiddle music, and are found in this piece. If this arrangement is too difficult for you, play the simplified version of this fiddle medley (without double stops). The term double stop simply mean a chord of two notes is played at the same time, and to do this, evenly place your bow on the two required strings as you pull your bow.

This fiddle medley begins with an excerpt from *Bile them cabbage down*. It features the shuffle bow stroke. Another fiddle technique you may want to try adding are slides. A sample slide is notated in the last measure of the piece, and is written the way it should sound (slide your finger from a low C natural to a C#). For fun, you may want to add more slides. For example, in *Bile them cabbage down*, you could add a slide on the first beat of measures 1, 2, 3 and 5, 6 and 7. During the section of the medley featuring *Devil's Dream*, play the fast sixteenth notes separately in the upper third of your bow. The final *Shuffle* section of the piece uses a simplified version of a double shuffle bowing stroke.

SECTION 6.12

PIECE: IRISH WASHERWOMAN

Irish Washerwoman is an Irish fiddle tune. It is in the musical form of a double jig, and it is a fast and lively dance. It is difficult to trace the actual origin of many British tunes, and although *Irish Washerwoman* is often considered to be an Irish tune, there are some who say it developed from an English country dance tune from 1688 called *Country Courtship*.[137] Regardless of its origins, *Irish Washerwoman* has a lilting, lively melody, and the rhythm plays a key role in the sound of the piece. The meter of the piece is in 6/8, and the notes are grouped into two sets of eighth notes. As you play this jig, slightly emphasize the first beat of each group of eighth notes in the following manner: ONE-two-three-FOUR-five-six. Although the piece is fast, you could try adding a few ornaments such as grace notes.

SECTION 6.13

RAGTIME

Ragtime is one of the precursors of jazz (it later merged with jazz). This style of popular music emerged around the turn of the twentieth century, and describes music with a ragged or syncopated rhythm. Syncopation is a term that means the music has an irregular feel to the rhythm, and this is generally achieved when the musical accent is shifted from a strong beat to a weak one (producing rhythmic patterns with unexpected accents).[138]

It is significant to mention that the syncopated rhythms of ragtime and many elements of blues and jazz are based on the folk music and rhythms of black Americans, many of whom were forcibly brought to America as slaves. Some of the forms of music contributing to blues and jazz included the improvised work songs of slaves called field hollers, and call and response songs. Field hollers were a plaintive, spontaneous solo by a worker. Call and response songs involved a leader calling out a line of text (using a musical form of rhythmic speech), which was then answered by the other workers in unison. The text of these work songs often centered around personal misfortune or how hard the work was; basically, complaints about the challenges of life and how the singer felt "blue." The concept of call and response was later used in jazz for instrumentalists to alternate musical exchanges back and forth.

Other music contributing to blues and jazz included the music sung by black religious congregations: gospel hymns, also called spirituals for "spiritual hymns." Spirituals frequently used the call and response technique and syncopated rhythms. Another form of music contributing to early forms of jazz took place in the mid-1800s, when plantation slaves would imitate the ballroom promenades of their masters in a dance called the cakewalk (it was more of a march than a dance). Dressed in fancy clothes, the slaves would use strutting, high and exaggerated steps and kicks, and were accompanied by a march with syncopated rhythms. The best stepping couple would often win a cake, thus this form of dance was called cakewalk. The ragged, syncopated rhythms used in these plantation cakewalk dances eventually became known as ragtime music.[139] [140]

One of the most prominent early composers of ragtime music, was Scott Joplin (1868-1917). Joplin was the son of a violin playing former slave (his mother was not a slave), and was one of the first black Americans to become a prominent composer. Some of Joplin's most popular compositions were his piano rags (rag means a piece composed in the style of ragtime). Joplin is often called the "King of Ragtime Writers," and his *Maple Leaf Rag* sold half a million copies by 1909.[141]

SECTION 6.14

PIECE: RAGTIME VIOLIN

Fig. 6.4 *The Ragtime Violin*

Another composer who profited from ragtime was Irving Berlin (1888-1989). Berlin, the son of a Jewish cantor, was self-taught as a musician, and one of his first big hits was the 1911 song *Alexander's Ragtime Band*. Berlin had a very successful 54 year career as a composer. In addition to composing sheet music in New York, he also wrote music for stage productions and scored music for Hollywood movies. A few of his notable works include the music for "God Bless America," (he was awarded a congressional gold medal for this), the music for the musical "Annie Get your Gun" (1946), and music for movies such as *White Christmas* (1954) and *There's No Business Like Show Business* (1954).[142]

TECHNIQUE TIPS: Irving Berlin wrote *Ragtime Violin* in 1911, and scored it for voice and piano. This arrangement features an instrumental melodic part with accompaniment, and the light and bouncy syncopated rhythm clearly makes it in the style of ragtime. Notice how this arrangement begins with an up-bow—this is designed to help with the flow and rhythm of the piece. After you've played through the piece, as an experiment, try starting with a down-bow, and play the first line. See if you notice any difference in being able to musically express the syncopated feel of the rhythm when you start the piece with a down-bow instead of an up-bow.

Ragtime Violin (lyrics):

Verse 1: Mister Brown, Mister Brown had a violin, Went around, all around with his violin. Lawdy, how he play'd it, sway'd it, made it moan so beautiful; Anna Lize, Anna Lize heard his violin, Roll'd her eyes, roll'd her eyes at his violin, Lawdy, how he lov'd 'er, turtled doved 'er, When Anna would cry.

Chorus: Fiddle up, fiddle up on your violin, Lay right on it, rest your chin upon it, Doggone you better begin, And play an overture upon your violin; Hurry up, hurry up with your violin, Make it sooner, don't you stop to tune 'er, Fid, fid, fid, fiddle the middle of your ragtime violin.

Verse 2: Mister Brown, Mister Brown at a fancy ball, Sat around, sat around, sat around the hall. Wouldn't take a chance to dance, because the band was terrible; Anna Lize, Anna Lize hit upon a plan, Roll'd her eyes, roll'd her eyes at the leader man, Took his fiddle down to Mister Brown, to Just kiss him and cry. (Chorus again)

SECTION 6.15

PIECE: THE CASTLE WALK

The syncopated element of ragtime began to be used in social dancing, particularly in dances such as the One Step (a fast march with syncopated rhythm). The One Step was a ballroom dance that became popular around 1910, largely due to the efforts of Vernon and Irene Castle, a husband and wife team who were renowned in Europe and the United States for their social dancing (they owned a dance studio called The Castle House). One of the variations of the One Step was called the Castle Walk, and it was invented by the Castles[143] (the Castles are featured on the front cover of the sheet music in figure 6.5).

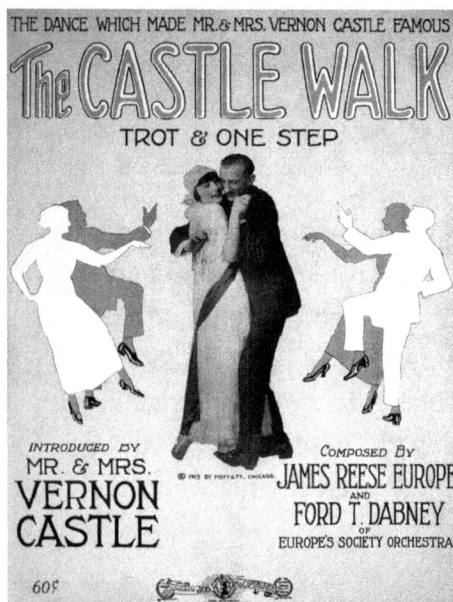

Fig. 6.5 *The Castle Walk Sheet Music*

The Castle Walk was composed in 1913 by James Reese Europe (1880-1919), and Ford Dabney (1917–19). Europe was a bandleader and composer, and made significant contributions towards the emergence of jazz. At one point in his career, Europe was the musical director for Vernon and Irene Castle. This partnership apparently had a dramatic impact on social dance in America, and the scholar Reid Badger noted: "the Castle-Europe partnership revolutionized American attitudes towards social dancing."[144] Europe frequently collaborated with Dabney, a songwriter and bandleader (Dabney also played piano in Europe's dance orchestras). Europe and Dabney composed the piece *The Castle Walk* for the Castles, and the Castle's used it to introduce their dance variation of the One Step, the Castle Walk. Europe also has the distinction of being one of the first black bandleaders to record with a major record label in the United States. Europe and his Society Orchestra received a recording contract from Victor Records in 1913, and one of the pieces recorded at Europe's 1914 second session at Victor Records, was *The Castle Walk*.[145] [146]

TECHNIQUE TIPS: *The Castle Walk* has the rhythmic, syncopated feel of ragtime music. The tempo marking at the beginning of this arrangement is *con spirito*, meaning play with spirit in a lively, animated manner. In measures 45-47, there is a *spicatto* section. *Spiccato* is an off-the-string, controlled bouncing bow stroke which produces a crisp sound and very short notes. To perform this bow stroke, try to find a spot on your bow where you're able to produce a controlled, light bounce (try starting in the middle).

SECTION 6.16

BLUES

William Christopher Handy (1873-1958), a composer, bandleader and publisher of blues music, is often credited with the title "Father of the Blues," and although some question if he truly deserves this honor, Handy clearly played an important role in helping the blues become a popular and mainstream part of American music. One of Handy's first hits was a piece he wrote in 1912 called *Memphis Blues*. *Memphis Blues* incorporated blue notes and the 12-bar blues progression with the syncopated musical style of ragtime, and although Handy was not the first musician to blend ragtime with the blues, from this point on, this style of music became extremely popular.[147]

Some of the characteristics of blues music include: the syncopated rhythms of ragtime; texts that deal with the melancholy side of life; an expressive vocal and instrumental style that frequently includes slides between pitches; the call and response pattern from the work songs of slaves; and the use of blue notes and familiar patterns such as the 12-bar blues. Blue notes are produced by lowering or flatting the third, seventh, and sometimes the fifth of a major scale. An example of a blues scale is found below.

Blues Scale

A 12-bar blues pattern typically has three four-measure phrases. The first two phrases often have the same melody, with a different third phrase (in instrumental music, the third phrase often consists of improvisation by the soloist). Other commonly used blues patterns include the 8-bar, and 16-bar blues.

SECTION 6.17

PIECE: ST. LOUIS BLUES

Handy's most successful composition was *St. Louis Blues*, composed in 1914. It is an enduring classic, and is still performed by jazz musicians today. According to the American Society of Composers, Authors and Publishers (ASCAP), it was the second most recorded song in the first half of the 20th century (the Christmas song "Silent Night" was first).[148] One of the unique features of this piece, was Handy's use of the Habanera rhythm in the bass part (he later used this rhythm with other blues pieces).

Here's an example of the Habanera rhythm, the same Afro-Cuban rhythm used in Bizet's Carmen:

Habanera Rhythm

Handy used both the twelve-bar blues pattern and the 16-bar blues pattern in creating this piece. He divided the piece into three sections: two 12-bar blues sections with the same melody, a minor 16-bar blues section utilizing the habanera rhythm, and a concluding 12-bar blues section. As you play this piece, you may want to try adding a few slides (for example, you could add slides to the "blue" notes—slide in and out of them). You also may want to interpret the rhythm freely, and let the eighth notes "swing," such as interpreting the eighth notes with a triplet feel in the following "swing rhythm" manner:

Swing Rhythm

St. Louis Blues Lyrics (*1st verse and chorus*)

I hate to see de ev'nin' sun go down
Hate to see de ev'nin' sun go down
'Cause, my baby, he done lef dis town

Feelin' tomorrow lak Ah feel today
Feel tomorrow lak Ah feel today
I'll pack my trunk Make ma get away

St. Louis woman wid her diamon' rings
Pulls dat man roun' by her apron strings
'Twant for powder an' for store bought hair
De man I love would not gone nowhere

Got de St. Louis Blues
Jes as blues as Ah can be
Dat man got a heart lak a rook cast in the sea
Or else he wouldn't have gone so far from me
(spoken – Dog-gone-it!)

SUMMARY

Additional stringed instrument styles. This unit has provided only a brief selection of non-traditional styles of string playing. There are many additional alternative uses of stringed instruments in a variety of musical styles, and just a few of these are jazz, hip-hop and rock. These styles often experiment with new performance techniques, amplify their instruments, and sometimes use electric violins, violas and cellos. Alternative styles merit more in-depth attention, as do all of the styles presented in this style sampler, and future study courses will present a more comprehensive treatment of specific styles of string music.

GLOSSARY

A tempo In tempo. "A tempo" is used after some variation in the tempo, and means return to the original tempo or speed.

Accelerando Accelerate or gradually increase the tempo or speed of the music.

Accent An accent placed over or under a note means the note should be emphasized by playing forcefully. Indicated by the sign: >

Accidentals A sign indicating a momentary departure from the key signature by using a flat, sharp or natural to temporarily alter the pitch of a note by a half step. Accidentals apply to the note immediately following the symbol, and remain in effect throughout the measure in which it appears.

Adagio A slow, leisurely tempo, often considered to be slower than andante, but not quite as slow as largo. Slow movements of a piece are sometimes titled Adagio.

Agitato Agitated or restless. Agitato is a direction to play in an agitated manner.

Air A melody, tune or song. In fiddle music, airs are often played slowly with rubato, and are not dance tunes.

Aleatory Comes from the Latin term alea, meaning "a game of dice." Aleatory music is also called chance music. Chance or indeterminancy may affect compositional elements, the performance, or both. For example, the performers may throw dice to determine compositional elements such as rhythmic or pitch choices.

Allegretto A lively and moderately fast tempo. Often considered to be slower than allegro, but faster than andante.

Allegro A quick, lively and fast tempo (not quite as fast as presto).

Amore Play with love, lovingly.

Andante A moderately slow tempo. Often considered to be a walking speed.

Andantino A slightly slower tempo than andante (andante is a moderately slow tempo).

Animando Play with increasing animation, liveliness, and expression.

Animato "Animated" or spirited. Play in a lively, spirited manner.

Appassionato Play passionately or with intense emotion and feeling.

Arco Arco is Italian for bow. After a pizzicato (plucked) section of music, arco is often used to indicate the next passage of music should be played with the bow.

Aria An elaborate vocal solo with instrumental accompaniment, used in genres such as an opera, oratorio or cantata.

Articulation Articulation describes the manner of providing definition and shape to individual notes or phrases. For string players, this involves both the right and left hand. The main markings are a dot . which means shorten the note, a line _ or slur ⌒ which means play the note smoothly, and an accent > which means add a forceful emphasis. These markings are often used in combination with each other, and mean many different things to different musicians.

Assai Assai means "very" in Italian. It modifies other terms when added to them, *e.g.* allegro assai means very fast.

Assez *Assez* means "enough" or "rather" in French. It modifies other terms when added to them, *e.g. assez vif* means "rather lively" in French (*vif* means lively), and *assez vite* means "rather fast" (*vite* means fast).

Atonality Music with an absence of tonality. Traditional tonal structures are intentionally ignored or abandoned in this contemporary form of music.

Au talon *Talon* is French for frog, and the term *au talon* is used in sections of music which should be played with the bow at the frog (other terms for frog include nut or heel).

Augmented Augmented means raised, and when the term augmented is combined with a specific interval between notes, it means to raise the interval by a half-step. For example, an augmented fourth is a half-step larger than the interval of a perfect fourth.

Ballata A *ballata* is a 14th century Italian secular song. It is a monophonic composition often in the following pattern: **A b b a A**.

Bariolage *Bariolage* is a French term which means an "odd mixture of colors," and directs the string player to achieve a contrast in tone colors by playing on different strings. An example of *bariolage* is when the same note is played, alternating between open strings and stopped strings, or by playing a repeated passage and oscillating between two, three, or four strings. Fingering is often used to indicate *bariolage*.

Binary Binary means dual or two parts.

Blue notes When the third, fifth, or seventh notes of a major scale are flattened, these notes are called blue notes. Blue notes are frequently used in blues and jazz music

Bow lift The sign for a bow lift is: ❟ and indicates the string player should lift their bow, and return it to its starting point.

Bravura Play brilliantly with boldness and spirit. The term *bravura* is sometimes used in passages where virtuosic skill is required of the performer.

Breve Short.

Brio Spirited and lively. *Con brio* means play with spirit in a vivacious manner.

Caccia *Caccia* means chase or hunt, and describes a canonic form of music, often with two voices chasing each other with an underlying third part. Hunting music themes were often used in this form of music.

Cantabile *Cantabile* means singing, and is a musical direction to play in a singing vocal style.

Cantata The term cantata means "to be sung" (as opposed to sonata, an instrumental work which means "to be played"). A cantata is a vocal work with instrumental accompaniment. It may be sacred or secular, and often contains sections such as solos, choruses, and recitatives.

Chamber music The term chamber music describes music suitable for performance in a chamber, meaning a room or small hall instead of a large concert hall. Today, chamber music is used to describe instrumental music performed by a small ensemble such as a quartet, trio or chamber orchestra.

Coda An Italian word for "tail," *coda* is a musical term referring to a concluding section of a composition.

Col legno "With the wood." *Col legno* means to strike the string with the stick of the bow rather than the hair (it is also called *col legno battuto*). When there are extended *col legno* passages in music, some professional violinists use inexpensive bows to avoid damaging their expensive bows. *Col legno tratto* is a less commonly used bowing direction. It indicates draw the wood of the bow across the string (use with caution, this can damage the wood of the bow).

Collé *Collé* means glued. It is a very short stroke, and begins with the bow lightly contacting the string with a distinct and short, sharp pinch. The bow is then lifted to prepare for the next stroke.

Comodo *Comodo* is Italian for a comfortable, leisurely and convenient tempo or speed, neither too fast nor too slow.

Con *Con* means "with" or in a style expressive of a certain quality. It is often used to modify another term such as *con spirito*, meaning to play with a spirited style.

Concerto grosso An instrumental concerto for a small group of soloists (called the *concertino*), which play in contrast to the main body of instrumentalists or orchestra (called the *ripieno* or *tutti*).

Concerto An instrumental composition for solo instrument(s), often in three movements, frequently accompanied by an orchestra. The sequence of the movements in a concerto generally is fast-slow-fast.

Continuo Also known as basso continuo or figured bass, the term continuo describes a bass part in a composition, often with numbers over the notes to indicate harmonic intervals that should be played above the bass line. During the Baroque period, the figured bass or continuo was commonly used by a keyboard player such as a harpsichord to provide harmonic accompaniments (a cello frequently played the continuo part along with the harpsichord).

Crescendo *Crescendo* (*cresc.*) means to gradually become louder, and is indicated by the sign:

Da capo (D.C.) repeat from the beginning.

Da segno (D.S.) repeat from the sign.

D.C. al Coda means go back to the beginning of the piece, play to the *Coda* sign: **⊕**, then jump to the *Coda* section to finish the piece (*Coda* means "tail," and refers to a concluding section of a piece).

D.C. al Fine means go back to the beginning, and end at the Fine marking (D.C. is an abbreviation for *da capo*, and means "from the beginning" and *Fine* means "end").

Détaché *Détaché* indicates a smooth, separate bow stroke should be used for each note (it does not mean detached or disconnected). Notes are of equal value, and are produced with an even, seamless stroke with no variation in pressure.

Détaché lancé *Détaché lancé* is a variation of the *détaché* bow stroke, and is a slightly separated bow stroke that gently articulates the notes with an unaccented, distinct break between each note. It is often used in combination with the *louré* or *porté* stroke to perform several separated notes in the same bow. A combination of a line with a dot over or under it is often used to indicate this bowing.

Diminuendo *Diminuendo* (*dim.*) means to gradually become softer. The term *decrescendo* (*decresc.* or *decr.*) also means to become softer, and is indicated by the sign:

Dolce *Dolce* is a direction to play sweetly, softly and gently.

Down bow The sign for down bow is ⊓ and indicates a downward stroke of the bow from frog to tip.

Drone A drone is a continuous pitch, held for an extended time beneath the melody to serve as an aural reference point. In early music, drones generally were not notated in manuscripts, so performers should use their judgment in using them. In fiddle music, drones are often played as double stops, with the fiddler playing a drone on one string, while playing the melody on another.

Dynamics A term that indicates the degree of loudness or softness in music. When the dynamic level is changed instantaneously, it is called terraced or changed dynamics (this was popular during the Baroque period). When the Italian word "issimo" is added to a dynamic term, it means very, extremely, or as much as is possible. *e.g.* pianissimo means "as soft as is possible" and fortissimo means "as loud as is possible."

Fermata The sign ⌢ under or over a note or rest indicates the note or rest should be held and prolonged at the discretion of the performer or conductor (this sign is also called a "hold" or by the nickname "bird's eye").

First and second endings First and second endings are repeat signs, and should be played as follows: play the first ending the first time through the music, repeat to the beginning of the section, then skip over the first ending and play the second ending.

Flautando *Flautando* is a bowing direction to bow slightly over the fingerboard to produce a flutelike sound effect.

Forte *Forte* means loud, and is indicated by the marking: $\boldsymbol{f}$

Fortissimo *Fortissimo* means the music should be very loud, and is indicated by the marking: $\boldsymbol{ff}$

Fortississimo *Fortissississimo* means the music should be played as loudly as possible, and is indicated by the marking: $\boldsymbol{fff}$

Fuoco *Fuoco* means "Fire" and indicates the musician should play with fire in a fiery, spirited manner.

Glissando Glissando is an ornamental effect notated by a wavy or straight line between two notes, indicating a continuous slide in pitch.

Grace note A grace note is used to ornament a note, and is written in a small font indicating the musician should quickly play the grace note, then the note it is attached to (the grace note is not part of the rhythmic value of the measure).

Grandioso Play with majestic grandeur.

Grave Play in a slow and solemn manner.

Harmonics Harmonics are overtones of the string and produce soft flutelike sounds when the string is lightly touched at specific fractional divisions (nodal points). Natural harmonics are produced on open strings, and artificial or stopped harmonics are produced on stopped strings.

Harmony Harmony is created when pitches are combined simultaneously.

Homophonic A form of musical texture with a melody and chordal accompaniment.

Hornpipe A lively British dance, popular during the 16th–18th centuries. The country dance version of the hornpipe was similar to the jig, but with a different meter (often in 3/2). Composers frequently used the lively country dance rhythm of the hornpipe dance for movements in dance suites and incidental theater music. Other meters used in the hornpipe dance were 2/4 and 4/4.

Impressionism Impressionism began as an artistic movement, and was used to describe a style of art which was designed to convey an impression rather than a literal depiction of the scene. This term was applied to music, particularly to compositions written by French composers in the early 20th century such as Debussy and Ravel when they wrote music that sought to convey subtle impressions, moods and emotions through compositional techniques such as new chord combinations, sonorities and harmonies, colorful instrumentation, and exotic scales.

Incidental music Music supplementing a spoken drama such as music composed for a play. Incidental music could be introducing a play (such as an overture), between acts (an interlude), or as a supplement to spoken parts or dramatic elements.

Jeté *Jeté* means "thrown" in French. In this bow stroke, the bow is thrown on the string, and then bounces for several notes in the same bow direction. The height and speed of the bounce are regulated through factors such as the amount of pressure used by the index finger, and where the bow is initially thrown or placed. Dots above or under the notes may be used to indicate *jeté*.

Largamente Play with a large, broad and sustained tone.

Larghetto Slightly faster than *largo*, *larghetto* is a similarly broad, large and stately tempo and style.

Largo A broad, slow tempo that is dignified and stately in style. *Largo* is the slowest of tempo markings.

Legato *Legato* indicates the notes should be smoothly connected, played either in one or several bows. Slurs are often used to indicate *legato*.

Lento *Lento* means slow in Italian (lent in French). *Lento* and *lent* are both slow tempos in between *largo* and *andante*.

Louré *Louré* strokes are a short series of gently pulsed legato notes executed in one bow stroke (it is also known as *portato*).

Madrigal A madrigal is an Italian song form, often with Italian text. It is a short work in one movement, sung by a small group of vocalists. Madrigal texts were often set to music using word painting (where the melody would follow the line of the text, *e.g.* waterfall would have music in the contour of falling water).

Maestoso Majestic and dignified.

Marcato An Italian term which means marked or accentuated.

Martelé *Martelé* is a French term meaning hammered. Each note is percussive, and commences with a sharp accent or "pinch" at the beginning of the note, followed by a quick release. *Martelé* may be notated in more than one way: with dots, hammer heads or accents.

Mass The Mass is the principal act of worship of the Catholic Church. As a vocal form, the Mass has been used in almost all periods of music history. It has two basic parts—the Proper and the Ordinary. Sections of the Mass that vary from day to day in each musical service are called the Proper. The Ordinary of the Mass consists of sections that are constant for every Mass. The fixed order of the Ordinary of the Mass is 1) Kyrie, 2) Gloria, 3) Credo, 4) Sanctus, and 5) Agnus Dei. The text of the Mass is given either as a Low Mass or High Mass. A Low Mass involves spoken text, while a High Mass is sung.

Meno *Meno* means less. It often is used with other terms such as *meno mosso* (less rapid or less motion).

Meter The grouping of beats in stressed and unstressed patterns.

Mezzo forte Moderately loud. *Mezzo forte* is indicated by the marking: **_mf_**

Mezzo piano Moderately soft. *Mezzo piano* is indicated by the marking: **_mp_**

Mode Modes are often used to structure the melody or tonality of a piece, and are comprised of notes arranged in a specific scale or pattern of intervals.

Moderato *Moderato* means to play at a moderate tempo or speed. This term sometimes modifies others such as *Allegro moderato*, which means moderately fast.

Modo ordinario *Modo* means "manner" or "style" and ordinario means ordinary. *Modo ordinario* means play in the ordinary way (often used after an unusual way of playing such as *col legno*).

Monophony Monophony is a musical texture for a single melodic line without any accompaniment or other melodic lines.

Mosso *Mosso* means moved. When used alone as a tempo term, the meaning of mosso is similar to con moto: with motion. *Mosso* is sometimes used with other qualifying terms such as *piu mosso*, meaning a little faster (more motion).

Motet Motet generally means a vocal piece with sacred text, musically composed in the style of the period. During the 13th-15th centuries, motets were sacred, unaccompanied choral works, often based on a preexisting melody and text. New melodies were then added to the preexisting melody, usually in counterpoint. Beginning in the 16th century, the preexisting melody frequently was secular.

Motive A short melodic or rhythmic idea that recurs throughout a musical composition.

Moto Moto means motion. It is often used with other terms such as con moto (with motion).

Multiple stops Multiple stops describe chords played on a stringed instruments. For example, double stops describe playing notes simultaneously on two strings, and triple stops mean playing notes simultaneously on three strings.

Muted A direction for the musician to play with a mute. For string players, mutes are small clamps of wood, metal, rubber, leather or plastic, which fit onto the bridge and result in a softer, muted sound with a veiled quality. To mute something is also indicated by the Italian term *con sordino* or the German term *mit dampfer*. The terms arco (bow), *via sordini* (take off mute) and *senza sordino* (without mute) are used to indicate when the muted section ends and the musician should resume playing with a bow.

Notation The writing down of musical notes and symbols to represent pitch, rhythm, and melodies.

Office The regular round of prayer and worship in monastic communities.

Opera A musical form of drama, originating in Italy, set to music. In an opera, most or all of the text is sung, using musical forms such as arias, songs, recitatives, duets, and choruses, with instrumental accompaniment. A few of the various subcategories of opera include heroic or grand opera, comedy opera and comic opera.

Oral tradition Oral tradition means that music is passed down from one musician to another orally, instead of through notated music.

Oratorio An oratorio is a large musical work, generally based on a sacred text or religious topic, with soloists, chorus and orchestra. Although many musical elements of an oratorio are similar to opera, no costumes, sets or acting are used, and oratorios are usually performed as a concert.

Ordinario *Ordinari*o or ord. means ordinary, and is used to indicate a return to ordinary playing after playing a special effect such as *col legno* or *sul ponticello*.

Ostinato Ostinato means "obstinate" in Italian. An ostinato is a short musical pattern, *e.g.* a melodic, rhythmic or harmonic figure, persistently repeated throughout a composition. A melodic pattern set in the bass is called basso ostinato (and is also known as ground bass).

Patronage A system of employment for musicians whereby a composer agreed to exclusive employment under the "auspices" of a patron. Patrons often were wealthy aristocrats or the church.

Phrase A musical idea or passage of music that is short, continuous and unbroken; similar to a musical sentence.

Pianissimo Very soft. *Pianissimo* is indicated by the marking: **pp**

Pianississimo As soft as possible. *Pianississimo* is indicated by the marking: **ppp**

Piano Soft. *Piano* is indicated by the marking: **p**

Pitch Pitch is the relative "highness" or "lowness" of a sound when compared with other notes. It can also indicate an absolute fixed position in a range of musical notes (*e.g.* the pitch "middle C").

Piu More.

Pizzicato *Pizzicato* (*pizz.*) is a term that means the string is plucked with the finger instead of being bowed.

Plainchant Also known as plainsong, chant or Gregorian Chant. Plainchant is a single melody, sung in unison by a soloist or choir, often using Latin words and a liturgical text.

Poco *Poco* means "little" or slightly. *A poco a poco* means little by little or gradually. *Poco* modifies other terms when added to them such as *poco diminuendo*, meaning to become slightly softer.

Polyphony Polyphony is a form of musical texture with several interdependent, overlapping melodic lines.

Portamento Portamento is an expressive device, and is a slide from one pitch to another.

Prelude A prelude is a piece which often serves as a musical introduction or prelude to a larger musical work (it sometimes is a short, independent instrumental piece in one movement).

Presto A fast, rapid and lively tempo, faster than *allegro*.

Program music Instrumental music which represents extra-musical concepts such as emotions, scenes or events through the music, not through words. It is also sometimes called descriptive music.

Punta d'arco *Punta d'arco* is a bowing direction to bow at the point or tip of the bow (punta means point, and arco means bow).

Quasi *Quasi* means "as if," "almost," or "nearly." It is often used to modify terms *e.g. allegretto quasi andantino*, meaning an *allegretto* tempo almost at an *andantino* tempo.

Rallentando *Rallentando* means gradually becoming slower. It also is abbreviated as *rall*.

Recitative A speechlike, declamatory form of singing used in vocal works such as operas, oratorios, and cantatas. Recitatives are often characterized by rhythmic freedom.

Religioso Play in a devotional or religious style.

Repeat Signs. A double bar with two dots is a repeat marking, and indicates the music in between the repeat signs should be repeated. If there is only one repeat sign with the dots facing to the left, go back to the beginning and play the entire section of music again (for more repeat sign variations, see *Da capo, da segno, D.C. al Fine, D.C. al Coda*, and first and second endings).

Requiem A Requiem Mass is a Mass for the dead.

Ricochet *Ricochet* is a bow stroke where the bow is dropped on the string and rebounds (bounces) on the string for several notes in the same bow direction.

Riff A riff is a short, repeated melodic pattern, and is often used in jazz.

Risoluto Resolutely; play in a resolute and decisive manner.

Ritardando Gradually become slower and slower (the same meaning as *rallentando*). *Ritardando* is often abbreviated as *rit*.

Rondeau A French musical term used during the Baroque era to describe a musical composition with a main section or theme which alternates with subsidiary sections or themes. This musical form was later expanded during the Classical era to become the musical form Rondo.

Rubato Rubato means "robbed." It refers to a temporary robbing of time by either slowing or speeding the tempo or rhythmic value of notes in a passage of music.

Sautillé *Sautillé* is a fast, bouncing or springing stroke in which the bow naturally bounces off of the string, producing a lighter, more rapid, and less percussive sound than *spiccato*.

Scale An ascending or descending arrangement of pitches.

Scherzo The term scherzo literally means "joke." In music, it is used to either describe an instrumental piece with a light, humorous character, or the second or third movement of a symphony or quartet (in place of the minuet). Scherzos often have a quick triple meter, a vigorous rhythm and a sharply contrasting harmony.

Scordatura Scordatura means abnormal tuning, and indicates one or more strings should be tuned higher or lower than usual (specific tuning directions for the new pitches are generally provided).

Semplice Simply. *Semplice* means to perform in a simple, unadorned, natural manner.

Sforzando *Sforzando* means forced or accented, and is usually attached to a single note or chord. It generally indicates the note should be played loudly with a sudden, accented emphasis, and is indicated by the marking:

sfz

Simile In a similar manner. Simile is often used to indicate a passage of music should be performed in the same manner as a preceding section.

Slur A slur is a curved line grouping notes together, and means the notes included in the slur should be played in the same bow ⌒. Unless otherwise indicated, notes in the slur should be played legato (smoothly). When slurs are used with dots over or under the notes, this indicates a slight separation should be used between the notes (the terms slurred staccato or dotted slurs are often used to describe this technique). When a slur is placed between two notes with the same pitch, this is called a "tie" and the two notes are played in one bow for the duration of both notes.

Sonata The word sonata comes from the Italian word *sonore*, meaning "to be played" (as opposed to cantata, a vocal work which means "to be sung"). A sonata is an instrumental form of music, and describes a multi-movement work for an instrument, often with accompaniment. The term has had varied meanings during different music eras, and during the Baroque period, the trio sonata was one of the most popular forms of sonata (often for two violins and continuo). During the Classical period, sonata came to mean a multi-movement work for a solo instrument with piano accompaniment, or piano alone.

Sonata form Sonata form is often used in the first movement in multi-movement works such as symphonies. It consists of an exposition section, followed by a development section, and concludes with a recapitulation.

Spiccato Spiccato is an off-the-string, controlled bouncing bow stroke which produces a crisp sound and very short notes. It is the slowest of the bouncing strokes. Dots above or under the notes may be used to indicate spiccato.

Staccato Staccato indicates the bow should remain on the string to play shortened and detached notes, distinctly separate from successive notes. Staccato is sometimes used with slurs (slurred staccato) for a series of short, stopped notes played in the same up or down bow (many violinists perform slurred staccato as a series of slurred *martelé* strokes).

String Quartet A string quartet is a composition for four stringed instruments: two violins, a viola and a cello. String quartet music generally is composed in a multi-movement form. The term string quartet is also used to describe a performance group comprised of four stringed instruments.

Suite A suite may be described as a collection of pieces, put together in an ordered manner. During the Baroque era, pieces in a suite were often dance forms such as: prelude, allemande, courante, saraband, gigue, bourre, gavotte, and minuet. After the Baroque era, suites were generally pieces extracted from a larger work such as *The Nutcracker Suite*, a compilation of pieces taken from the ballet *The Nutcracker*.

Sul *Sul* means "on the" or "near the." *Sul* is used in terms such as *sul tasto* (bow over or near the fingerboard), *sul ponticello* (bow near the bridge), or *sul G* (play on the G string and only the G string until otherwise indicated). In violin music, when only a specific string should be used for particular passages, *sul* is sometimes used with numerals such as *sul IV* to indicate only one string should be used (G, the fourth string, is indicated by the numeral IV, A is III, D is II and E is I).

Sul ponticello *Sul ponticello* is a bowing direction to play with the bow near the bridge. The result is a glassy, whispery sound.

Sul tasto *Sul tasto* is a bowing direction to bow over or near the fingerboard. The resulting sound is soft and flutelike (see *flautando*).

Syllabic In vocal music, syllabic, neumatic and melismatic are terms used to indicate whether the syllables of the text are sung to a single note (syllabic), several notes (neumatic), or many notes per syllable (melismatic).

Symphony A symphony is an extended composition for orchestra and is often comprised of three to five movements.

Symphonic Poem A symphonic poem is a programmatic orchestral work, often in one movement. It is also known as a tone poem. In a symphonic poem, extra musical ideas such as emotions, scenes or events, are expressed through the music, not through words.

Syncopation Rhythmic patterns with unexpected accents. Syncopation is generally achieved by shifting the musical accent from a strong beat to a weak one. This results in an irregular feel to the rhythm.

Tempo Tempo means the rate of speed or pace of the music. Tempo also may be used with other qualifying words such as *a tempo*, meaning return to the original tempo or speed. Various tempo markings are used to indicate directions for the rate of speed such as *andante* (moderately slow) and *allegro* (fast). Metronome markings are another way to specify even more precisely the tempo of music *e.g.* ♩ = 60 means each quarter note should be played at the speed of 60 quarter notes per minute.

Tempo di valse Play the music at the rate of speed or pace of a waltz.

Tenuto Tenuto means the note(s) should be played sustained or broadly, and held for its whole value. A line placed under or over the note is usually used to indicate tenuto: ＿.

Theme A theme is the main musical subject of a composition such as a melody, phrase or short motive.

Theme & variations A composition with a theme and variations of that theme.

Tie When a slur is placed between two notes with the same pitch, this is called a "tie" and the two notes are played in one bow for the duration of both notes.

Time Signature A sign or fraction placed at the beginning of a piece to show how many beats are in each measure. For example, a time signature of 3/4 indicates each measure contains three quarter notes.

Tremolo Tremolo means rapidly repeating a single note or chord (see bowing chart for more details).

Trill A trill ornaments a note, and is a rapid alternation between two pitches, usually a major or minor second above the note. The letters *tr* and a wavy symbol ♦♦ are used as trill markings. Accidentals are often used to indicate whether the trill is a major or minor trill.

Troppo *Troppo* means "too much." It is often used to modify other terms such as *Adagio ma non troppo*, meaning, slow but not too slow.

Turn Turns are ornaments mainly used in 17th-19th century music, and generally indicate four notes should be played, encircling the notated note. The following symbol for a turn is placed above the note: ∞.

Twelve tone technique The twelve tone technique refers to a system where the composer arranges the twelve notes of the chromatic scale in a fixed order. This ordered sequence of the twelve notes is called a twelve-tone row or series that forms a unique melody. Composers using this method generally would not repeat any note in the tone row until the entire series of twelve notes had been heard. Variations to the tone row include mathematical approaches such as retrograde, inverted and transposed versions of the tone row. The twelve-tone technique was later called serialism, and continues to be used by some composers today.

Up bow The sign for up-bow is V and indicates an upward stroke of the bow from the point (or tip) to the frog (or nut).

Vibrato Vibrato for stringed instruments is similar to vocal vibrato—it is a slight and rapid fluctuation in pitch, and is used to add warmth and expression to music. There are three types of vibrato: finger, hand, arm or a combination of all three. Variations in the width and speed of the vibrato can produce a wide range of expression.

Virtuoso Virtuoso means "exceptional performer" in Italian, and is used to describe a highly proficient, technically skilled performer. When the descriptive term virtuosic playing is used, it generally means the performer is playing difficult music in a highly skilled manner.

Vivace Lively and brisk. As a tempo marking, *vivace* is often considered slightly faster than *allegro*.

Waltz A dance in triple meter which was very popular during the late eighteenth and nineteenth centuries.

Whole Bow Initials are sometimes used in music to indicate what part of the bow should be used: WB = Whole Bow; LH = Lower Half; UH = Upper Half; MB = Middle of the Bow.

BOWING CHART

BOW STROKES: On the String*

NOTATION	NAME	DEFINITION
	Collé	Collé means glued. It is a very short stroke, and begins with the bow lightly contacting the string with a distinct and short, sharp pinch. The bow is then lifted to prepare for the next stroke. The resulting sound was described by Galamian as being similar to pizzicato with the bow. Although collé usually has no articulation markings, dots are sometimes used.
	Détaché	Détaché indicates smooth, separate bow stroke should be used for each note (it does not mean detached or disconnected). Notes are of equal value, and are produced with an even, seamless stroke with no variation in pressure.
	Détaché lancé	Détaché lancé is a variation of the détaché bow stroke. A slightly separated bow stroke is used to gently articulate the notes with an unaccented, distinct break between each note. It is often used in combination with the louré or porté stroke to perform several separated notes in the same bow.
	Legato	Legato indicates the notes should be smoothly connected, played either in one or several bows (slurs are often used with the legato bow stroke).
	Louré	Louré strokes are a short series of gently pulsed legato notes executed in one bow stroke (it is also known as portato). A slight swelling at the beginning of the note should be applied, followed by a gradual lightening of the sound. Strokes are distinctly separate, yet unaccented, and the expressive swell is produced by applying pressure and speed to the bow at the beginning of the note. Although a slur and horizontal dashes are generally used to indicate this effect, dots with slurs are occasionally used.
	Martelé	Martelé is a French term meaning hammered. Each note is percussive, and commences with a sharp accent or "pinch" at the beginning of the note, followed by a quick release. Before the bow is set in motion, the index finger applies this "pinch" or "bite" for articulation. Martelé may be notated in more than one way: with dots, hammer heads or accents.
	Staccato	Staccato indicates the bow should remain on the string to play shortened and detached notes, distinctly separate from successive notes. Staccato is sometimes used with slurs (slurred staccato) for a series of short, stopped notes played in the same up or down bow (many violinists perform slurred staccato as a series of slurred martelé strokes).

Articulation markings often mean different things. For example, a dot means shorten the note and can indicate bow strokes such as spiccato (off the string) and staccato (on the string). It is important to understand the context of the music and the purpose for the articulation in order to properly interpret the markings and corresponding bow strokes. It should also be noted that bowing terminology and markings are not always precise. Different bow strokes are often used in combination with other bow strokes to achieve the desired musical effect. Musicians sometimes disagree about how to interpret bowing terminology and markings, so use your best judgment, and enjoy the music!

BOW STROKES: *Off the String*

NOTATION	NAME	DEFINITION
	Jeté	Jeté means "thrown" in French. In this bow stroke, the bow is thrown on the string, and then bounces for several notes in the same bow direction. The height and speed of the bounce are regulated through factors such as the amount of pressure used by the index finger, and where the bow is initially thrown or placed.
	Ricochet	Ricochet is a bow stroke where the bow is dropped on the string and rebounds (bounces) on the string for several notes in the same bow direction. The natural resiliency of the string helps the bow to bounce. As in the jeté bow stroke, the height and speed of the bounce are regulated through factors such as additional pressure used by the index finger, and where the bow is initially thrown or placed. Although ricochet and jeté are similar, some violinists consider jeté to be more of a controlled bounce than ricochet (there are some violinists who use these terms interchangeably).
	Sautillé	Sautillé is a fast, bouncing or springing stroke in which the bow naturally bounces off of the string, producing a lighter, more rapid, and less percussive sound than spiccato. The natural resiliency of the bow is utilized to produce this light, fast stroke, and it is often played in the middle of the bow.
	Spiccato	Spiccato is an off-the-string, controlled bouncing bow stroke which produces a crisp sound and very short notes. It is the slowest of the bouncing strokes.

Additional Bowing Effects & Directions

NOTATION	NAME	DEFINITION
	Accent	An accent placed over or under a note means the note should be emphasized by playing forcefully.
	Arco	Play with the bow (bowing directions such as arco are often used after a plucked, pizzicato section).
	Au talon	Talon is French for frog, and this term means a particular section of music should be played with the bow at the frog (other terms for frog are nut or heel).
	Bariolage	Bariolage is a French term which means an "odd mixture of colors," and directs the string player to achieve a contrast in tone colors by playing on different strings. An example of barriolage is when the same note is played, alternating between open strings and stopped strings, or by playing a repeated passage, oscillating between two, three, or four strings. Fingering is often used to indicate bariolage.
	Bow lift	Lift the bow, and return to its starting point

	Col legno	"With the wood." Col legno means to strike the string with the stick of the bow rather than the hair (it is also called col legno battuto) When there are extended col legno passages in music, some professional violinists use inexpensive bows for these sections in order to avoid damaging their expensive bows. Col legno tratto is less commonly used, and indicates the wood of the bow should be drawn across the string (use with caution, this can damage the wood of the bow).
⊓	**Down bow**	Begin the bow at the frog, and pull the bow from the frog to the tip.
	Flautando	Bow slightly over the fingerboard.
	Punta d'arco	Bow at the point or tip of the bow.
sfz	**Sforzando**	Sforzando means forced or accented, and is usually attached to a single note or chord. It generally indicates the note should be played loudly with a sudden accented emphasis
	Slur	A curved line grouping notes together, indicating the notes included in the slur should be played in the same bow. Unless otherwise indicated, notes in the slur should be played legato. When slurs are used with dots over or under the notes, this indicates a slight separation should be used between the notes (the terms slurred staccato or dotted slurs are often used to describe this technique). When a slur is placed between two notes with the same pitch, this is called a "tie" and the two notes are played in one bow for the duration of both notes.
	Sul ponticello	Play with the bow near the bridge. The result is a glassy, whispery sound.
	Sul tasto	Bow over the fingerboard. This produces a soft, flutelike sound.
	Tenuto	Play sustained or broadly, and hold the note for its whole value.
	Tie	Connect two or more notes of the same pitch with one bow
	Tremolo (bowed tremolo)	Bowed tremolo indicates the note should be played with very short, rapid and unaccented bow strokes, moving the bow back and forth for the duration of the note value (tremolos are usually played in the upper third of the bow, and a light wrist motion is used to achieve them.) Tremolos are either measured (a clear subdivision of the note's rhythmic value) or unmeasured (play the note as fast as possible). Tremolo signs are indicated by short slanted lines through note stems. For example, one line through a stem indicates eighth note tremolos, 2 lines mean sixteenth note tremolos, and 3 lines indicate unmeasured tremolo. If tremolos are placed on a beamed note, the beam counts as one of the lines.

NOTATION	NAME	DEFINITION
	Tremolo (fingered tremolo)	Tremolos may also be played between more than one note, and this is called fingered tremolo (it is also known as slurred tremolo). Instead of the bow rapidly moving, the fingers rapidly alternate between the two notes of the interval, while the bow smoothly plays. Fingered tremolo is generally notated by incomplete beams being placed between two notes of an interval to indicate the rhythmic value of the tremolo.
V	**Up bow**	Begin the bow at the point or tip, and pull the bow from the point to the frog.
WB, LH, UH, MB	**Whole Bow**	These terms are sometimes used to indicate what part of the bow should be used: WB = Whole Bow; LH = Lower Half; UH = Upper Half; MB = Middle of the Bow

Additional Skills and Effects

NOTATION	NAME	DEFINITION
	Glissando	An ornamental effect notated as two notes connected by a wavy or straight line, indicating a continuous slide in pitch. Instead of playing the two notes separately, the finger should smoothly slide along the string between the two notes, playing all of the notes along the line in a subtle or pronounced manner (including the two notated notes). The context of the glissando should determine its interpretation.
	Grace note	Used to ornament a note, a grace note is written in a small font indicating the musician should quickly play the grace note, then the note it is attached to (the grace note is not part of the rhythmic value of the measure).
	Harmonics *(natural harmonics)*	Harmonics are overtones of the string and produce soft flutelike sounds when the string is lightly touched at specific fractional divisions (nodal points). Natural harmonics are produced on open strings, and artificial or stopped harmonics are produced on stopped strings. Composers often indicate which string should be used for the harmonic by notating above or below the note markings such as sul D, D string, or III (meaning, play the harmonic on the D string, the third string on the violin). Natural harmonics are indicated in two ways: by a small "o" written above the note to be lightly touched, and by a small diamond shape at a specific point on the string where the finger should be lightly placed. The most commonly used natural harmonics are described below, with notated examples on the D string 1) The string is divided in half (two equal parts). When the string is lightly touched in the middle, the resulting pitch sounds one octave above the open string. This particular harmonic is generally notated at the actual pitch with a small circle above it. Ex. 1 is an example of a natural harmonic dividing the string into one half on the D string. To play it, find the middle point of the D string (the indicated note D), and lightly touch this note with your finger. As you use your bow to play this note, the resulting pitch should be one octave above the open string D.

	Harmonics *(cont.)*	2) The string is divided in thirds (three equal parts). If the string is lightly touched at one third of the string length from either end, the resulting pitch should be an octave and a perfect fifth above the open note. Ex. 2 is an example of a natural harmonic dividing the string into thirds.
		3) The string is divided into fourths (four equal parts). If the string is lightly touched at one of the nodes dividing the string in fourths, the resulting pitch should be two octaves above the open string. Ex. 3 is an example of this harmonic:
		4) The string is divided into fifths (five equal parts). If the string is lightly touched at one of the nodes dividing the string in fifths, the resulting pitch should be two octaves and a third above the open string. Ex. 4 is an example of this harmonic:
	Harmonics (artificial harmonics)	Artificial or stopped harmonics are produced by firmly pressing the first finger down on a note two octaves below the desired pitch, and then lightly touching the fourth finger a perfect fourth above the notated pitch. This divides the string into fourths, similar to example 3 in natural harmonics. The resulting sound is two octaves above the stopped pitch. Less commonly used, are artificial harmonics with a lightly touched finger a third or fifth above the stopped notes.
		When artificial harmonics are notated, a small diamond shape is used to indicate the note that should be lightly touched. Ex. 5 is an example of an artificial harmonic on the D string, with the artificial harmonic a fourth above the notated pitch. To play it, firmly press your first finger down on the notated E, and lightly touch your fourth finger on the pitch A indicated by the diamond shape. The resulting sound should be two octaves above the stopped first finger E.
	Multiple stops	A collective term used to describe chords played on a stringed instruments. Specific terms for each chord include the following:
		1) double stop (a chord using two strings; play notes simultaneously on two strings);

	Multiple stops (cont.)	2) triple stop (play the chord using three strings);
		3) quadruple stop (play the chord using four strings). When performing triple stops and quadruple stops, the chords are often played either two at a time (bottom two notes of the chord, then the top two notes of the chord), or the notes are arpeggiated and played one note at a time as in the following example of an arpeggiated quadruple stop:
con sordino	**Muted**	Play with a mute. Mutes are small clamps of wood, metal, rubber, leather or plastic, which fit onto the bridge and result in a softer, muted sound with a veiled quality. Muted sections of music are also indicated by the German term mit dampfer. The terms arco (bow), via sordini (take off mute), or senza sordino (without mute), are used to indicate when the muted section ends and the musician should resume playing with a bow.
ordinario	**Ordinary**	Ordinario or ord. means ordinary, and is used to indicate a return to ordinary playing after playing a special effect such as col legno or sul ponticello.
(pizz.)	**Pizzicato** *(pizz.)*	Indicates notes should be plucked rather than bowed. Violinists usually play pizzicato with their right index finger. To do this, they often place their thumb. against the corner or side of the fingerboard to support the hand while plucking. A return to bowing is often indicated by the term arco. Less commonly used pizzicato effects are listed below.
	Left hand pizz.	Left hand pizzicato is indicated by the + sign placed over or under the note, and is sometimes used while the right hand continues to use the bow (it is generally played by plucking with the 4th finger of the left hand).
	Nail pizz.	Nail pizz. indicates the player should use their fingernail instead of the fleshy part of their finger to pluck the string. The result is a metallic sounding pizzicato (this form of pizz. is difficult for violinists since they generally keep their fingernails short).
quasi guitar	**Guitar Pizzicato**	Guitar pizzicato is indicated by the term quasi guitar, meaning the violin is held like a guitar and strummed.

	Pizzicato tremolo	Tremolo notation along with the term pizzicato, indicates the player should use pizzicato tremolo. To do this, the finger moves up and down, rapidly plucking the notes for a tremolo effect
	snap pizzicato	In snap pizzicato, the string is plucked with such force that it snaps against the fingerboard when released. Snap pizz. is often called "Bartok" pizzicato, since the composer Bartok frequently used it in his string music.
	Scordatura	Scordatura means abnormal tuning, and indicates one or more strings should be tuned higher or lower than usual (specific tuning directions for the new pitches are generally provided).
	Sul G **Sul D** **Sul A** **Sul E**	Sul G means play on the G string and only the G string until otherwise indicated. In violin music, it is sometimes notated Sul IV or simply the numeral IV over or under the music, since G is the fourth string on the violin. Sul D (or III, the third string on the violin), Sul A (or II, the second string on the violin) and sul E (or I, the first string on the violin) also mean to play the notes on the single string indicated.
	Trill	A trill ornaments a note, and is a rapid alternation between two pitches, usually a major or minor second above the note. Accidentals are often used to indicate whether the trill is a major or minor trill.
	Turn	Turns are ornaments mainly used in music from the 17th-19th century. A turn generally indicates four notes should be played, encircling the notated note such as in the example provided:
	Vibrato	Cello vibrato is similar to vocal vibrato—it is a slight and rapid fluctuation in pitch, and is used to add warmth and expression to music. Louis Potter Jr., the author of *The Art of Cello Playing,* suggested that the vibrato unit for cello consists of the forearm, wrist, hand and the playing finger. Potter defined cello vibrato as: "The cello vibrato is a bouncing, somewhat rotary movement back and forth, parallel to the fingerboard, produced by the left forearm from the elbow, with the wrist acting only as a part of the whole vibrato unit (*The Art of Cello Playing,* p. 108).

REFERENCES

UNIT 1- EARLY VIOLIN ENDNOTES

[1] Schlesinger, Kathleen. "Cithara," *The Encyclopedia Britannica.* 11th Edition, Ed. Hugh Chisolm. New York: Encyclopedia Britannica, 1910: 395-397.

[2] Bachmann, Werner. *The Origins of Bowing.* London: Oxford University Press, 1969: 25, 33-34.

[3] Remnant, Mary. "Rebec," *The New Grove Dictionary of Music and Musicians.* ed. Stanley Sadie. London: Macmillan, 1980. 15: 635.

[4] Dilworth, John. "The Violin and Bow—Origins and Development," *The Cambridge Companion to the Violin.* ed. Robin Stowell. Cambridge University Press, 1992: 5.

[5] Dilworth, John. "The Cello: Origins and Evolution," *The Cambridge Companion to the Cello.* ed. Robin Stowell. Cambridge University Press, 1999: 7.

[6] Hoppin, Richard. *Medieval Music.* New York: W.W. Norton & Co., 1978: 349-352.

[7] Gushee, Lawrence. "Minstrel," *The New Grove Dictionary of Music and Musicians.* ed. Stanley Sadie. London: Macmillan, 1980. 12: 348.

[8] Newman, Barbara. *Sister of Wisdom.* Berkeley: University of California Press, 1987: 11.

[9] Hildegard of Bingen. *Scivias*, Book III, Vision 13/16, 1151.

[10] McGee, Timothy. *Medieval Instrumental Dances.* Bloomington: Indiana University Press, 1989: 26, 164.

[11] Lockwood, Lewis. "Estampie," *The New Grove Dictionary of Music and Musicians.* ed. Stanley Sadie. London: Macmillan, 1980. 6: 254.

[12] Greer, David. "Henry VIII," *The New Grove Dictionary of Music and Musicians.* ed. Stanley Sadie. London: Macmillan, 1980. 8: 485-486.

[13] Dean-Smith, Margaret. "Jig," *The New Grove Dictionary of Music and Musicians.* ed. Stanley Sadie. London: Macmillan, 1980. 9: 648.

[14] Dart, Thurston and Tilmouth, Michael. "Jigg," *The New Grove Dictionary of Music and Musicians.* ed. Stanley Sadie. London: Macmillan, 1980. 9: 649.

[15] Holman, Peter. *Four and Twenty Fiddlers.* Oxford University Press, 1993: 4-5, 39, 103.

[16] *The New Grove Violin Family.* ed. David D. Boyden et al. New York: W.W. Norton, 1989: 175-82.

[17] *The Cambridge Companion to the Cello.* ed. Robin Stowell. Cambridge University Press, 1999: 92-159.

[18] *The New Grove Violin Family.* 1989: 144-48.

[19] Riley, Maurice. *The History of the Viola.* Ann Arbor, Michigan: Braun-Brumfield, 1980: 70-74.

[20] Jennings, John. "Lupo," *The New Grove Dictionary of Music and Musicians.* ed. Stanley Sadie. London: Macmillan, 1980. 11:336.

[21] Holman, 1993: 79-83, 108-109.

[22] Holman, 1993: 89, 186, 213.

[23] Field, Christopher; Helm, Eugene; Drabkin, William. "Fantasia," *The New Grove Dictionary of Music and Musicians.* ed. Stanley Sadie. London: Macmillan, 1980. 6: 380.

[24] Zaslaw, Neil. "The Italian Violin School in the 17th Century," *Early Music*, 18, 1990: 515.

[25] Boyden, David D. *The History of Violin Playing from Its Origins to 1761 and Its Relationship to the Violin and Violin Music.* London: Oxford University Press, 1965: 4.

[26] Dart, Thurston and Coates, William, eds. "Jacobean Consort Music." *Musica Britannica*, vol. 9. London: Stainer & Bell, 1966: xv.

[27] Price, David C. *Patrons and Musicians of the English Renaissance.* Cambridge: Cambridge University Press, 1981: 47.

[28] Boyden, 1965: 245.

[29] Stowell, Robin. "The Pedagogical Literature," *The Cambridge Companion to the Violin.* ed. Robin Stowell. Cambridge University Press, 1992: 277.

[30] Stowell, 1992: 225.

[31] Crome, Robert. *The Fiddle New Model'd, or a Useful Introduction for the Violin, Exemplify'd with Familiar Dialogues.* London: J. Tyther, c. 1740, Preface.

[32] Crome, Robert. *The compleat tutor for the violoncello, containing the best & easiest instructions for learners* London: C.S. Thompson, c.1763-1776.

UNIT 2 - BAROQUE MUSIC ENDNOTES

[1] Holman, Peter and Thompson, Robert. "Henry Purcell II," *Grove Music Online* (Accessed 20 August 2007) <http://www.grovemusic.com>

[2] Cole, Malcolm S. "Rondeau," *The New Grove Dictionary of Music and Musicians.* ed. Stanley Sadie. London: Macmillan, 1980. 16:170.

[3] Dean-Smith, Margaret. "Hornpipe," *The New Grove Dictionary of Music and Musicians.* ed. Stanley Sadie. London: Macmillan, 1980. 8:721.

[4] Dean, Winton and Hicks, Anthony. "George Frideric Handel," *The New Grove Dictionary of Music and Musicians.* ed. Stanley Sadie. London: Macmillan, 1980. 8:83-140.

[5] Thompson, Clyde H. "Marin Marais," *The New Grove Dictionary of Music and Musicians.* ed. Stanley Sadie. London: Macmillan, 1980. 11:640-41.

[6] Talbot, Michael. "Arcangelo Corelli," *The New Grove Dictionary of Music and Musicians.* ed. Stanley Sadie. London: Macmillan, 1980. 4:768-774.

[7] Palisca, Claude V. *Baroque Music.* Englewood Cliffs, New Jersey: Prentice Hall, 1991: 154-155.

[8] Mangsen, Sandra; Irvine, John; Rink, John; and Griffiths, Paul. "Sonata," *Grove Music Online* (Accessed 21 August 2007) <http://www.grovemusic.com>

[9] Talbot, Michael and Ryom, Peter. "Antonio Vivaldi," *The New Grove Dictionary of Music and Musicians.* ed. Stanley Sadie. London: Macmillan, 1980. 20:31-46.

[10] Hudson, Richard. "Folia," *The New Grove Dictionary of Music and Musicians.* ed. Stanley Sadie. London: Macmillan, 1980. 6:690-692.

[11] Walker, Thomas. "Variations," *The New Grove Dictionary of Music and Musicians.* ed. Stanley Sadie. London: Macmillan, 1980. 19:536-45.

[12] Talbot, Michael and Ryom, Peter. "Antonio Vivaldi," *The New Grove Dictionary of Music and Musicians.* ed. Stanley Sadie. London: Macmillan, 1980. 20:31-46.

[13] Michael Talbot. "Vivaldi's Op. 5 Sonatas," *The Strad*. Vol. 90, 1980: 678.

[14] Boyden, David D. *The History of Violin Playing from its Origins to 1761*. London: Oxford University Press Inc., 1965: 399.

[15] Wolf, Christoph and Jones, Richard. "Johann Sebastian Bach," *The New Grove Dictionary of Music and Musicians*. ed. Stanley Sadie. London: Macmillan, 1980. 1:785-840.

[16] Bonta, S.; Campbell, M.; Kernfeld, B.; and Barnett, A. "Violoncello," *Grove Music Online*. (Accessed 7 June 2008) <http://www.grovemusic.com>

[17] Wolf, Christoph and Jones, Richard. "Johann Sebastian Bach," *The New Grove Dictionary of Music and Musicians*. ed. Stanley Sadie. London: Macmillan, 1980. 1:785-840.

[18] *Bach-Dokumente*. Bach-Archiv Leipzig. Vol. 1, 1963-72: 206ff. quoted by Geck, Martin. *Johann Sebastian Bach: Life and Work*. translated by John Hargraves. New York: Harcourt, 2006: 106.

[19] Schnoebelen, Anne. "Maurizio Cazzati," *The New Grove Dictionary of Music and Musicians*. ed. Stanley Sadie. London: Macmillan, 1980. 4:40-42.

[20] Schnoebelen, Anne. "The Role of the Violin in the Resurgence of the Mass in the 17th Century," *Early Music*, Vol. 18, No. 4. Nov. 1990:541.

[21] Smither, Howard E. "Oratorio," *Grove Music Online*. (Accessed 21 August 2007) <http://www.grovemusiconline.com>

[22] Dean, Winton and Hicks, Anthony. "George Frideric Handel," *The New Grove Dictionary of Music and Musicians*. ed. Stanley Sadie. London: Macmillan, 1980. 8:83-140.

[23] Hicks, Anthony, "George Frideric [Georg Friederich] Handel [Händel, Hendel]," *Grove Music Online*. (Accessed 21 August 2008) <http://www.grovemusic.com>

[24] Timms, Colin; Fortune, Nigel and Boyd, Malcolm, et al. "Cantata," *Grove Music Online*. (Accessed 7 June 2008 <http://www.grovemusiconline.com>

[25] Zohn, Steven and Payne, Ian. "Bach, Telemann, and the Process of Transformative Imitation in BWV 1056/2 (156/1)," *The Journal of Musicology*, Vol. 17, No. 4. Autumn, 1999: 548.

UNIT 3 - CLASSICAL MUSIC ENDNOTES

[1] Sadie, Stanley and Hicks, Anthony. "Wolfgang Amadeus Mozart," *The New Grove Dictionary of Music and Musicians*. ed. Stanley Sadie. London: Macmillan, 1980: 12:680-752.

[2] Einstein, Alfred. *Mozart: His Character, His Work*. London: Oxford University Press, 1961:280.

[3] Bashford, Christina. "Chamber Music," *Grove Music Online*. (Accessed 11 June 2008) <http://www.grovemusic.com>

[4] Brown, Maurice J. E. and Sams, Eric. "Franz Schubert," *The New Grove Dictionary of Music and Musicians*. ed. Stanley Sadie. London: Macmillan, 1980. 16:752-811.

[5] Webster, James and Feder, Georg. "(Franz) Joseph Haydn," *Grove Music Online*. (Accessed 4 June 2008) <http://www.grovemusiconline.com>

[6] Thomas Mee Pattison (1845-1936), the composer of the original *Maidstone Violin Tutor* (London, c. 1897), was a musical advisor to the London-based J. G. Murdoch & Co., music publishing house and instrument manufacturer. Pattison enlisted the support of his company to promote violin class instruction for British schoolchildren by providing all of the supplies needed: violins, teaching materials, and teachers, for one inclusive, inexpensive price.

The Maidstone method of violin class instruction was named in honor of the first group violin class to experiment with this approach: the All Saints' National School in Maidstone, England (see "The Original Maidstone Class," *The Young Musician.* London: National Union of School Orchestras. Jan/Feb. 1910: 4). At the height of the Maidstone School Orchestra (MSOA) classes popularity, 400,000 British schoolchildren, one in ten of the British state school population, participated in Maidstone School Orchestra classes (see *School Music Review* Vol. 26/182: 21). In the United States, this early approach to group violin instruction is sometimes known as the Maidstone Movement, and American music educators were made aware of the Maidstone Movement and MSOA classes through the conference reports of individuals who had observed MSOA classes in person. One individual in particular was influential in disseminating the MSOA concept of group string classes: Albert G. Mitchell, one of the pioneers in American public school instrumental classes. Mitchell spent a year in England studying the methodology used by MSOA classes, and upon his return, patterned his 1911 Boston public school violin classes directly after MSOA classes. Mitchell's violin classes were soon included in the regular school curriculum, and he expanded his group instrumental classes to other instruments. Numerous music education historians in the United States regard the British Maidstone Movement as a significant event in the history of school instrumental music in the United States, and T. Mee Pattison was a key individual in beginning this widespread and influential British approach to group violin instruction. For more information, see: Deverich, Robin K. "The Maidstone Movement—Influential British Precursor of American Public School Instrumental Classes," *Journal of Research in Music Education.* Spring 1987: 39-55.

[7] Webster, James and Feder, Georg. "(Franz) Joseph Haydn," *Grove Music Online.* (Accessed 4 June 2008) <http://www.grovemusiconline.com>

[8] Griesinger, Georg August. *Biographical Notes of Joseph Haydn.* translated by Vernon Gotwals, in *Haydn Two Contemporary Portraits.* Madison: The University of Wisconsin Press, 1968:33.

[9] Beethoven, Ludwig van. *Beethoven's letters (1790-1826).* translated by Lady Wallace. Freeport, New York: Books for Libraries Press, 1970.

[10] Kerman, Joseph and Tyson, Alan. "Beethoven," *Grove Music Online.* (Accessed 12 June 2008) http://www.grovemusic.com

UNIT 4 - ROMANTIC MUSIC ENDNOTES

[1] Head, Matthew. "Style hongrois," *Grove Music Online.* (Accessed 12 June 2008) <http://www.grovemusic.com>

[2] Bozarth, George and Frisch, Walter. "Johannes Brahms," *Grove Music Online.* (Accessed 12 June 2008) <http://www.grovemusic.com>

[3] Tyrrell, John. "Proksch, Joseph," *Grove Music Online. Oxford Music Online.* (Accessed 11 Oct. 2008) <http://www.oxfordmusiconline.com>

[4] Mead, David Bruce. *The symphonic structure of Smetana's "Ma vlast."* D.M.A. dissertation, The University of Texas at Austin, 1994.

[5] Ottlová, Marta, and Tyrrell, John. "Bedřich Smetana," *Grove Music Online.* (Accessed 18 June 2008) <http://www.grovemusic.com>

[6] Tyrrell, John. "Bedřich Smetana," *Grove Music Online–Opera.* (Accessed 18 June 2008) <http://www.grovemusic.com>

[7] Horton, John and Grinde, Nils. "Edvard (Hagerup) Grieg," *Grove Music Online.* (Accessed 26 June 2008) <http://www.grovemusic.com>

[8] Bergsagel, John. "Ole (Bornemann) Bull," *Grove Music Online.* (Accessed 30 June 2008) <http://www.grovemusic.com>

[9] Neal, Mary Elizabeth. *Devil's instrument, national instrument: The Hardanger fiddle as metaphor of experience in the creation and negotiation of cultural identity in Norway*. Ph.D. dissertation, Indiana University, 1991.

[10] Bjorndal, Arne. "The Hardanger Fiddle: The Tradition, Music Forms and Style," *Journal of the International Folk Music Council*, Vol. 8. 1956: 13-15.

[11] Goertzen, Chris. *Fiddling for Norway: Revival and Identity*. Chicago: The University of Chicago Press, 1997: preface.

[12] Anderson, Rasmus Björn, and Moore, Aubertine Woodward. *The Norway music album: a selection for home use*. Boston: Oliver Ditson & Co, 1881: 77.

[13] Grinde, Nils. "Halling [parhalling]," *Grove Music Online*. (Accessed 30 June 2008) <http://www.grovemusic.com>

[14] Kemp, Peter. "Strauss," *Grove Music Online*. (Accessed 13 June 2008) <http://www.grovemusic.com>

[15] Lamb, Andrew. "Waltz," *Grove Music Online*. (Accessed 13 June 2008) <http://www.grovemusic.com>

[16] Kemp, Peter. "About the Music," *Vienna Philharmonic New Year's Concert 2008*. (Accessed 14 June 2008) <http://www.decca.com/newyearsconcert2008/aboutthemusic.html>

[17] Ard, Jamee, and Fitzlyon, April. "Viardot (Michelle Ferdinande) Pauline," *The Norton/Grove Dictionary of Women Composers*. eds. Julie Anne Sadie and Rhian Samuel. New York: W. W. Norton & Co., 1995:474-478.

[18] Harris, Rachel M. *The music salon of Pauline Viardot: Featuring her salon opera "Cendrillon."* D.M.A., Louisiana State University: 2005.

[19] Fitzlyon, April. "Pauline (Michelle Ferdinande) Viardot," *The New Grove Dictionary of Music and Musicians*. ed. Stanley Sadie. London: Macmillan, 1980. 19:694-695.

[20] Kimber, Marian Wilson. "The 'Suppression" of Fanny Mendelssohn: Rethinking Feminist Biography," *19th Century Music,* Fall 2002. Vol. 26, 2: 113-129.

[21] Todd, Larry R. "Mendelssohn(-Bartholdy), (Jacob Ludwig) Felix," *Grove Music Online*. (Accessed 20 August 2007) <http://www.grovemusic.com>

[22] Döge, Klaus. "Antonín (Leopold) Dvořák," *Grove Music Online*. (Accessed 14 June 2008) <http://www.grovemusic.com>

[23] Oldani, Robert William. "Aleksandr Porfir'yevich Borodin," *Grove Music Online* ed. L. Macy. (Accessed 16 June 2008) <http://www.grovemusic.com>

[24] Garden, Edward. "The Five" [Moguchaya kuchka; Mighty Handful]," *Grove Music Online*. (Accessed 16 June 2008) <http://www.grovemusic.com>

[25] Kauffman, George B. and Bumpass, Kathryn. "An Apparent Conflict between Art and Science: The Case of Aleksandr Porfir'evich Borodin (1833-1887)," *Leonardo*, Vol. 21, No. 4. *The MIT Press*, 1988: 429-436.

[26] Schwarz, Boris. "Aleksandr Konstantinovich Glazunov," *Grove Music Online*. (Accessed 16 June 2008) <http://www.grovemusic.com>

[27] Schwarz, Boris and Hibberd, Sarah. "Henry Vieuxtemps," *Grove Music Online*. (Accessed 16 June 2008) <http://www.grovemusic.com>

[28] Fine, Marshall. "The Unfinished Vieuxtemps Sonata and its Completion," *JAVS Online,* Summer 2003. (Accessed 16 June 2008), <http://www.americanviolasociety.org/JAVS%20Online/Summer%202003/Vieuxtemps/vieuxtemps.html>

[29] Huebner, Steven. "Charles-François Gounod," *Grove Music Online*. (Accessed 4 June 2008) <http://www.grovemusic.com>

[30] Tiersot, Julien and Baker, Theodore. "Charles Gounod: A Centennial Tribute," *The Musical Quarterly*, Vol. 4, No. 3. July, 1918: 413.

[31] Nectoux, Jean-Michel. "Gabriel (Urbain) Fauré," *Grove Music Online.* (Accessed 16 June 2008) <http://www.grovemusic.com>

[32] Stanichar, Christopher Michael. *Gabriel Faure's "Pelleas et Melisande."* D.M.A., University of Cincinnati, 1997.

[33] Little, Meredith Ellis. "Siciliana," *Grove Music Online.* (Accessed 21 August 2007) <http://www.grovemusic.com>

[34] Harris, Rachel M., 2005.

[35] MacDonald, Hugh. "Jules (Emile Frédéric) Massenet," *Grove Music Online.* (Accessed 18 June 2008) <http://www.grovemusic.com>

[36] Milnes, Rodney. "Jules (Emile Frédéric) Massenet," *Grove Music Online—Opera.* (Accessed 18 June 2008) <http://www.grovemusic.com>

[37] Milnes, Rodney. "Thaïs," *Grove Music Online—Opera.* (Accessed 18 June 2008) <http://www.grovemusic.com>

[38] MacDonald, Hugh. "Georges (Alexandre-César-Léopold) Bizet" *Grove Music Online* ed. L. Macy. (Accessed 18 June 2008) <http://www.grovemusic.com>

[39] Barulich, Frances. "Carmen," *Grove Music Online–Opera.* (Accessed 18 June 2008) <http://www.grovemusic.com

[40] MacDonald, Hugh. "Georges (Alexandre-César-Léopold) Bizet" *Grove Music Online–Opera.* (Accessed 18 June 2008) <http://www.grovemusic.com>

[41] Barulich, Frances. "Habanera," *Grove Music Online.* (Accessed 18 June 2008) <http://www.grovemusic.com>

[42] Wiley, Roland John. "Pyotr Il'yich Tchaikovsky," *Grove Music Online.* (Accessed 12 June 2008) <http://www.grovemusic.com>

UNIT 5 - 20TH CENTURY MUSIC ENDNOTES

[1] White, Eric Walter. *Stravinsky: The Composer and His Works.* Berkeley: University of California Press, 1979: 48.

[2] Whittall, Arnold, "Neo-classicism," *Grove Music Online.* (Accessed 21 June 2008), <http://www.grovemusic.com>

[3] Massine, Leonide. *My Life in Ballet.* ed. Phyllis Hartnoll and Robert Rubens. London: Macmillan, 1968: 128-129.

[4] Carson, Penelope Hummer. *Pulcinella and his Friends: Comic Origins of New-Classicism in Music for Diaghilev's Stage Works.* M.A. thesis, The American University, 1986.

[5] Paymer, Marvin E., and Williams, Hermine W., *Giovanni Battista Pergolesi: A Guide to Research.* New York: Garland Publishing, 1989: 8.

[6] Gallo's instrumental compositions were frequently sold using Pergolesi's name as the composer. For example, Pergolesi was attributed as the composer for Gallo's *Twelve Sonatas for Two Violins and a Bass* in the following London editions: 1771, printed "for Mr. Webb, etc.;" 1780, R. Bremmer; 1795, Preston and Son; 1894, J. Williams (see British Library catalogue for more editions).

[7] Brook, Barry S. "Stravinsky's Pulcinella: the 'Pergolesi' Sources." In *Musique signes images: Liber amicorum Francois Lesure,* edited by Joel-Marie Fauquet. Geneva: Minkoff, 1988: 41-66. cited by Paymer, 156.

[8] Paymer, ix.

[9] Brook, Barry S. "Pergolesi: Vindication after 250 Years," *The Musical Times,* Vol. 127, Mar., 1986: 141-145.

[10] *The Pergolesi Research Center* (Accessed 14 August 2008)
<http://web.gc.cuny.edu/BrookCenter/pergolesi.htm>

[11] Walsh, Stephen, "Igor (Fyodorovich) Stravinsky," *Grove Music Online.* (Accessed 21 August 2007)
<http://www.grovemusic.com>

[12] Calvocoressi, M. D., "Maurice Ravel," *The Musical Times*, Vol. 54, 1913: 785-787.

[13] MacDonald, Hugh, "Ravel and the Prix de Rome," *The Musical Times,* Vol. 116, 1975: 332-333.

[14] Kelley, Barbara L. "Ravel, "(Joseph) Maurice Ravel," *Grove Music Online.* (Accessed 26 August 2007)
<http://www.grovemusic.com>

[15] Bailey, Kathryn, "Anton (Friedrich Wilhelm von) Webern," *Grove Music Online.* (Accessed 27 June 2008)
<http://www.grovemusic.com>

[16] Shakers, officially known as United Society of Believers in Christ's Second Appearing, are a Protestant religious denomination that branched off from the Quakers in England, and emigrated to the United States in 1774. Only a handful of followers still practice this religion today. See Chase, Stacey. "The Last Ones Standing," *The Boston Globe,* July 23, 2006. (Accessed 29 June 2008)
<http://www.boston.com/news/globe/magazine/articles/2006/07/23/the_last_ones_standing/>

[17] Hall, Roger L. "Joseph Brackett's 'Simple Gifts'," *Shaker Music.* (Accessed 1 May 2008)
<http://www.americanmusicpreservation.com/shakermusic4.htm>

[18] Andrews, Edward Deming. *The Gift to be Simple: Songs, Dances and Rituals of the American Shakers.* New York, 1940.

[19] Yellin, Victor Fell and Hitchcock, Wiley, "American Shakers," *Grove Music Online.* (Accessed 28 June 2008),
<http://www.grovemusic.com>

[20] *Shaker Songs: A Musical Celebration of Peace, Harmony, and Simplicity.* Compiled and edited by Christian Goodwillie with contributions from Joel Cohen. New York: Black Dog & Leventhal Publishers, 2002.

[21] Pegg, Carole; Myers, Helen; Bohlman, Philip B.; and Stokes, Martin. "Ethnomusicology," *Grove Music Online.* (Accessed 30 June 2008), <http://www.grovemusic.com>

[22] Whitaker, Frank. "A Visit to Béla Bartók," *The Musical Times.* Vol. 67, No. 997. 1926: 220-223.

[23] Bartók, Béla and Dille, Denijs. "The Life of Béla Bartók," *Tempo,* New Series, No. 13, Autumn, 1949: 3-7.

[24] Bartok, Bela and Baker, Theodore. "Hungarian Peasant Music," *The Musical Quarterly,* Vol. 19, No. 3. 1933: 267-287.

[25] Gillies, Malcolm. "Béla Bartók," *Grove Music Online.* (Accessed 21 August 2007) http://www.grovemusic.com

UNIT 6 - NON-TRADITIONAL MUSIC ENDNOTES

[1] Wilkinson, Irén Kertész. "'Gypsy' [Roma-Sinti-Traveller] Music," *Grove Music Online.* (Accessed 20 August 2007) <http://www.grovemusic.com>

[2] Shapiro, Michael. "They Call Themselves Roma," *Roots World* (Accessed 9 May 2007)
<http://www.rootsworld.com/rw/gypsypage.html>

[3] Glass, Herbert, "Romany life: What is the Gypsy idiom?" *Opera News*. New York: Mar. 16, 1997. Vol. 60, 13: 18-21.

[4] Nickson, Chris. "Roma (Gypsy) Music," *National Geographic*. (Accessed 1 July 2008) <http://worldmusic.nationalgeographic.com/worldmusic/view/page.basic/genre/content.genre/roma__gypsy__music_778>

[5] Malvinni, David. *The Gypsy Caravan: From Real Roma to Imaginary Gypsies in Western Music and Film*. New York: Routledge, 2004: 377.

[6] Bartók, Béla. "Gypsy Music or Hungarian Music?" *The Musical Quarterly*, Vol. 33, No. 2. Apr., 1947: 240-257.

[7] Kovalcsik, Katalin. "Popular Dance Music Elements in the Folk Music of Gypsies in Hungary," *Popular Music*, Vol. 6, No. 1. Jan., 1987: 45-65.

[8] Frigyesi, Judit. "Béla Bartók and the Concept of Nation and 'Volk' in Modern Hungary," *The Musical Quarterly*, Vol. 78, No. 2. Summer, 1994: 255-287.

[9] Feldman, Walter Z. "Bulgărească/Bulgarish/Bulgar: The Transformation of a Klezmer Dance Genre," *Ethnomusicology,* Vol. 38, No. 1. Winter, 1994: 1-35.

[10] Netsky, Hankus. "An Overview of Klezmer Music and its development in the U.S," *Judaism*. Winter, 1998: 5-12.

[11] Feldman, Walter Zev. "Klezmer (Jewish Music, Non-liturgical instrumental music)," *Grove Music Online*. (Accessed 20 August 2007) <http://www.grovemusic.com>

[12] Netsky, Hankus. "American Klezmer: A Brief History," *American Klezmer : its Roots and Offshoots,* ed. by Mark Slobin. Berkeley: University of California Press, 2002: 14.

[13] Solomon, Sophie. "Klezmer Violin Technique," *The Strad*. Jan., 2007: 62-65.

[14] Horowitz, Josh. "The Main Klezmer Modes," *Klezmer Shack*. (Accessed 9 May 2007) <http://www.klezmershack.com/articles/horowitz/horowitz.klezmodes.html>

[15] Feldman, 1994: 1.

[16] Chianis, Sotirios. "Greece, Folk Music," *The New Grove Dictionary of Music and Musicians*. ed. Stanley Sadie. London: Macmillan, 1980. 7: 675.

[17] Mathiesen, Thomas J. et al. "Greece," *Grove Music Online*. (Accessed 21 August 2007) <http://www.grovemusic.com>

[18] "Traditional Stringed Instruments of Greece," *Hellenic Communication Service*. (Accessed 5 July 2008) <http://www.helleniccomserve.com/stringintruments.html>

[19] Magrini, Tullia. "Repertories and identities of a musician from Crete," *Ethnomusicology OnLine Symposium on Mediterranean Musicians*. (Accessed 2 August 2007) <http://www.research.umbc.edu/eol/3/magrini/index.html>

[20] Ibid.

[21] Raphael, Souzana. "The Hidden Treasure: Traditional Music in Greece," *Matt Barrett's Greece Travel Guide*. (Accessed 5 July 2008) <http://www.greecetravel.com/music/traditional.html>

[22] "Greece: Mapping the Sounds of Folk Music," *The Garland Encyclopedia of World Music Online*. Vol. 8: Europe, ed. Timothy Rice, James Porter, and Chris Goertzen: 2000. (Accessed 6 February 2009) <http://glnd.alexanderstreet.com>

[23] Holden, Rickey and Vouras, Mary. *Greek Folk Dances*. Newark, New Jersey: Folkraft Press, 1965: 9.

[24] Patsidou, Lena. "Greek Dancing Through the Centuries: the history and evolution of Greek dance," *Research on the History of Greek Dance* (Accessed 5 July 2008) <http://www.annaswebart.com/culture/dancehistory/>

[25] Stratou, Dora. *Greek Folk Dances.* Greece: National Greek Folk Dances and Songs Society, 1965.

[26] Crosfield, Domini. *Dances of Greece.* New York: Chanticleer Press, 1948.

[27] Aguilar n.d.:125-26, in Járuregui 1990:18, quoted by Daniel Sheehy in *Mariachi Music in America.* Oxford: Oxford University Press, 2006: 15.

[28] Béhague, Gerard; Chamorro, Arturo and Stanford, E. Thomas. "Mexico, Traditional Music: Mestizo forms," *Grove Music Online.* (Accessed 6 May 2007) <http://www.grovemusic.com>

[29] Henriques, Donald Andrew. *Performing nationalism: Mariachi, media and transformation of a tradition (1920--1942)* Ph.D. dissertation, The University of Texas at Austin, 2006.

[30] Clark, Jonathan D. "A Brief History on the Mariachi Tradition," *The Latino Encyclopedia.* New York: Marshall Cavendish Corp, 1996. *Mariachi Publishing Company* (Accessed 15 May 2007) <http://www.sobrino.net/mer/entry_on_the_word_mariachi.htm>

[31] Mendoza, Vicente T. and Fraser, Norman. "The Frontiers between 'Popular' and 'Folk.'" *Journal of the International Folk Music Council*, Vol. 7. 1955: 24-27.

[32] Sobrino, Laura. "Analyzing Mariachi Traditional and Popular Song Forms," *Mariachi Publishing Company* (Accessed 17 May 2007) <http://www.mariachipublishing.com>

[33] Sheehy, Daniel Edward; Olsen, Dale A. "Mexico," *The Garland Encyclopedia of World Music Online.* Volume 2: South America, Mexico, Central America, and the Caribbean. ed. Dale A. Olson and Daniel E. Sheehy. Routledge: 1998. (Accessed 19 July 2008) <http://glnd.alexanderstreet.com>

[34] "Jarabe Tapatio," *Danzas y Trajes Tipicos de Jalisco. Gobierno de Jalisco, Secretaria de Cultura.* (Accessed 11 July 2008) <http://cultura.jalisco.gob.mx/danzaytraje/jtapatio.html>

[35] Medina, Notario Antonio García. "Mariachi, Son y Jarabe," *Ensayo cultural: Revista Digital de Derecho, Colegio de Notarios de Jalisco, Mexico* (Accessed 11 July 2008) <http://www.revistanotarios.com/?q=node/17>

[36] Fuld, James J. *The Book of World-Famous Music.* New York: Dover Publications, Inc., 1985: 366-67.

[37] "The Mexican Hat Dance," *Mexican Folkloric Dance Company of Chicago.* (accessed 6 May 2008) <http://www.mexfoldanco.org/jarabe.shtml>

[38] "The Mexican Hat Dance," *Mexican Folkloric Dance Company of Chicago.* (accessed 6 May 2008) <http://www.mexfoldanco.org/jarabe.shtml>

[39] Díaz, Alicia. "Dance and Dance Forms," *The Oxford Encyclopedia of Latinos and Latinas in the United States.* Suzanne Oboler and Deena J. González, Oxford University Press 2005. *Oxford Reference Online.* Oxford University Press. (Accessed 11 July 2008) <http://www.oxfordreference.com>

[40] "Jarabe *(noun),*" *The Oxford Essential Dictionary of Foreign Terms in English.* ed. Jennifer Speake. Berkley Books, 1999. *Oxford Reference Online.* Oxford University Press. (Accessed 11 July 2008), <http://www.oxfordreference.com>

[41] "Zapateado *(noun)*" *The Oxford Essential Dictionary of Foreign Terms in English.* ed. Jennifer Speake. Berkeley Books, 1999. *Oxford Reference Online.* Oxford University Press. (Accessed 11 July 2008) <http://www.oxfordreference.com>

[42] "China," *The Garland Encyclopedia of World Music Online*. Vol. 7: East Asia: China, Japan, and Korea. ed. Robert C. Provine, Yosihiko Tokumaru, and Lawrence Witzleben. Routledge: 2001. (Accessed 18 July 2008) <http://glnd.alexanderstreet.com>

[43] Han, Kuo-Huang. "Folk Songs of the Han Chinese: Characteristics and Classifications," *Asian Music*, Vol. 20, No. 2, Chinese Music Theory. Spring-Summer, 1989: 107-128.

[44] Thrasher, Alan R. et al. "China," *Grove Music Online. Oxford Music Online.* (Accessed 18 Jul. 2008) <http://www.oxfordmusiconline.com>

[45] Provine, Robert C.; Tokumaru, Yosihiko and Witzleben, J. Lawrence. "China: A Musical Profile," *The Garland Encyclopedia of World Music Online*. Vol. 7: East Asia: China, Japan, and Korea. ed. Robert C. Provine, Yosihiko Tokumaru, and Lawrence Witzleben. Routledge: 2001. (Accessed 18 July 2008) <http://glnd.alexanderstreet.com>

[46] Jones, Stephen. "Source and Stream: Early Music and Living Traditions in China," *Early Music*, Vol. 24, No. 3, Early Music from Around the World. Aug., 1996: 375-388.

[47] Thrasher, Alan R. "The Melodic Structure of Jiangnan Sizhu," *Ethnomusicology,* Vol. 29, No. 2. Spring-Summer, 1985: 237-263.

[48] Ibid.

[49] Lu-Ting, Ho and Kuo-huang, Han. "On Chinese Scales and National Modes," *Asian Music*, Vol. 14, No. 1. 1982: 132-154.

[50] Yingshi, Chen; Provine, Robert C.; Tokumaru, Yosihiko and Witzleben, J. Lawrence, "Theory and Notation in China," *The Garland Encyclopedia of World Music Online*. Vol. 7: East Asia: China, Japan, and Korea. ed. Robert C. Provine, Yosihiko Tokumaru, and Lawrence Witzleben. Routledge: 2001. (Accessed 18 July 2008) <http://glnd.alexanderstreet.com>

[51] Thrasher, Alan R. "The Melodic Structure of Jiangnan Sizhu," *Ethnomusicology,* Vol. 29, No. 2. Spring-Summer, 1985: 254.

[52] Liu, Terence Michael. *Development of the Chinese Two-Stringed Bowed Lute 'Erhu" Following the New Culture Movement (c. 1915-1985).* Ph.D. dissertation, Kent State University, 1988.

[53] Stock, Jonathan. "A Historical Account of the Chinese Two-Stringed Fiddle Erhu," *The Galpin Society Journal*, Vol. 46. March 1993: 83-113.

[54] Stock, Jonathan. "Erhu," *Abing, His Life and His Music.* (Accessed 7 July 2008) <http://www.shef.ac.uk/music/staff/js/AbErhu.html>

[55] Stock, Jonathan P.J. "Liu Tianhua." *Grove Music Online. Oxford Music Online.* (Accessed 18 Jul. 2008) <http://www.oxfordmusiconline.com>

[56] Wu, Ben; Provine, Robert C.; Tokumaru, Yosihiko and Witzleben, J. Lawrence, "Archaeology and History of Musical Instruments in China," *The Garland Encyclopedia of World Music Online*. Vol. 7: East Asia: China, Japan, and Korea. ed. Robert C. Provine, Yosihiko Tokumaru, and Lawrence Witzleben. Routledge: 2001. (Accessed 18 July 2008) <http://glnd.alexanderstreet.com>

[57] Micic, Peter. "The Jasmine Crossing," *Danwei* (Accessed 17 May 2008) <http://www.danwei.org/music/the_jasmine_crossing_by_peter.php>

[58] Lim, Louisa. "Chinese Composer Gives 'Turandot' a Fresh Finale," *NPR* (Accessed 17 May 2008) <http://www.npr.org/templates/story/story.php?storyId=90037060&ft=1&f=1105>

[59] Quershi, Regula, et al. "India," *Grove Music Online. Oxford Music Online.* (Accessed 13 Jul. 2008) <http://www.oxfordmusiconline.com>

[60] Powers, Harold S. "India," *The New Grove Dictionary of Music and Musicians.* ed. Stanley Sadie. London: Macmillan, 1980. 9: 69-141.

[61] "The Classical Traditions," *The Garland Encyclopedia of World Music Online.* Vol. 5: South Asia: The Indian Subcontinent, ed. Alison Arnold. Routledge: 2001. (Accessed 13 October 2008) <http://glnd.alexanderstreet.com>

[62] Swift, Gordon. "Ornamentation in South Indian Music and the Violin," *Carnatic Corner* (Accessed 21 August 2007) <http://www.www.carnaticcorner.com/articles/violin_technique_article.pdf>

[63] Swift, Gordon. *The Violin as Cross-cultural Vehicle: Ornamentation in South Indian Violin and Its Influence on a style of Western Violin Improvisation.* Ph.D. dissertation, Wesleyan University, 1989.

[64] Wade, Bonnie. *Music in India.* New Delhi: Manohar, 2004.

[65] Krishnan, G.J.R. "The Rise of Violin in the South-Adaptation at its Best," Paper presented at the *The Chembur Fine Arts Society* in Mumbai, India, Feb. 1999 (Accessed 5 February 2009) <http://www.carnatica.net/sangeet/gjrviolin.htm\>

[66] Lord, Maria. "Tyāgarāja." *Grove Music Online. Oxford Music Online.* (Accessed 13 Jul. 2008) <http://www.oxfordmusiconline.com>

[67] Swift, Gordon. "Exploring Carnatic Violin," *Strings*, Feb. 2005: 63-67.

[68] Racy, Ali Jihad. "Arab Music," *The Genius of Arab Civilization: Source of Renaissance.* ed. John Hayes. New York University Press, 1992.

[69] Marcus, Scott. "The Interface between Theory and Practice: Intonation in Arab Music," *Asian Music,* Vol. 24, No. 2. Spring-Summer, 1993: 39-58.

[70] Marcus, Scott. *Arab Music Theory in the Modern Period.* Ph.D. dissertation, UCLA, 1989: 161-240.

[71] Touma, Habib Hassan. *The Music of the Arabs.* Portland, Oregon: Amadeus Press, 1996: 47.

[72] Wright, Owen; Poché, Christian; and Shiloah, Amnon. "Arab Music," *Grove Music Online.* (Accessed 8 August 2007) <http://www.grovemusic.com>

[73] Racy, 1992.

[74] Racy, Ali Jihad. "The Many Faces of Improvisation: The Arab Taqāsīm as a Musical Symbol," *Ethnomusicology*, Vol. 44, No. 2. Spring-Summer, 2000: 308.

[75] Racy, 1992.

[76] Racy, Ali Jihad. *Making Music in the Arab World.* Cambridge: University Press, 2003: 77.

[77] Juma, Rashed. *A Guide to Arabic Violin Technique for the Classical Violinist.* D.M.A. dissertation, University of Miami, 2002: 17-18.

[78] Wright, "Arab Music."

[79] "Arabic Musical Forms: The Longa," *Maqam World.* (Accessed 15 July 2008) <http://www.maqamworld.com/forms.html>

[80] Rosenberg, Neil V. "The Classification of Traditional Instrumental Music," *The Journal of American Folklore*, Vol. 108, No. 428. Spring, 1995: 188.

[81] Stokes, Martin. "Tanburi Cemil Bey." *Grove Music Online. Oxford Music Online.* (Accessed 16 July 2008) <http://www.oxfordmusiconline.com>

[82] "Tanburi Cemil Bey," *Türk Mûsikîsi.* (Accessed 15 July 2008) <http://www.turkmusikisi.com/bestekarlar/tanburicemilbey.htm>

[83] Tanrikorur, Cinuçen. "The Ottoman Music," translated by Dr. Savaş Ş. Barkçin *Türk Mûsikîsi* (Accessed 16 July 2008) <http://www.turkmusikisi.com/osmanli_musikisi/the_ottoman_music.htm>

[84] Walter Zev Feldman. "Ottoman music," *Grove Music Online. Oxford Music Online.* (Accessed 16 Jul. 2008) <http://www.oxfordmusiconline.com>

[85] Reel, James. "Learning Arabic: Leanne Darling offers an Introduction to this Vibrant Musical Style," *Strings.* November 2006: 28-29.

[86] Juma, 2002: 19-24.

[87] Remnant, Mary. "Fiddle," *Grove Music Online.* (Accessed 20 August 2007) <http://www.grovemusic.com>

[88] Remnant, Mary and Goertzen, Chris. "Hardanger fiddle," *Grove Music Online. Oxford Music Online.* (Accessed 19 July 2008) <http://www.oxfordmusiconline.com>

[89] Montagu, Jeremy. "Fiddle," *The Oxford Companion to Music.* ed. Alison Latham. *Oxford Music Online.* (Accessed 19 July 2008) <http://www.oxfordmusiconline.com>

[90] "Spike fiddle," *Grove Music Online. Oxford Music Online.* (Accessed 19 July 2008) <http://www.oxfordmusiconline.com>

[91] Djedje, Jacqueline Cogdell. *Fiddling in West Africa.* Bloomington, Indiana: Indiana University Press: 2008.

[92] Haigh, Chris. *Fiddling Around the World.* (Accessed 21 July 2008) <http://www.fiddlingaround.co.uk>

[93] Hebert, Donna. "The reel deal," *Strings.* May-Jun. 2002, Vol. 16, 8: 28-31.

[94] Lieberman, Julie Lyonn. *Alternative Strings: the New Curriculum.* Cambridge: Amadeus Press, 2004.

[95] Lieberman, Julie Lyonn. *The Contemporary Violinist.* New York: Huiksi Music, 2005.

[96] Goertzen, Chris, Wilgus, D.K., and Crawford, Richard et al. "United States of America," *Grove Music Online. Oxford Music Online.* (Accessed 22 Jul. 2008) <http://www.oxfordmusiconline.com>

[97] Rosenberg, Neil V. "Bluegrass music," *Grove Music Online. Oxford Music Online.* (Accessed 24 Jul. 2008) <http://www.oxfordmusiconline.com>

[98] "A Brief History of Cajun, Creole, & Zydeco Music," *LSUE's Central Acadiana Gateway.* (Accessed 24 July 2008) <http://www.lsue.edu/acadgate/music/history.htm>

[99] Olsen, Dale A. "An Ethnomusicological Survey of the Cajuns of Louisiana: An Introduction to Cajun Music and Culture," *Ethnomusicology as Advocacy.* (Accessed 24 July 2008) <http://mailer.fsu.edu/~dolsen/advocacy/Cajun/cajun.htm>

[100] "Cajun music," *The Oxford Companion to Music.* ed. Alison Latham. *Oxford Music Online.* (Accessed 24 Jul. 2008) <http://www.oxfordmusiconline.com>

[101] "Cajun Music," *Encyclopedia of Cajun Culture.* ed. Shane K. Bernard. (Accessed 24 July 2008) <http://web.archive.org/web/20051213013220/www.cajunculture.com/Other/cajun.htm>

[102] Burman-Hall, Linda C. "Southern American Folk Fiddle Styles," *Ethnomusicology.* Vol. 19, No. 1. Jan., 1975: 47-65.

[103] Graf, Sharon Poulson. *Traditionalization at the National Oldtime Fiddlers' Contest: Politics, power, and authenticity.* Ph.D. dissertation, Michigan State University, 1999.

[104] Malone, Bill C. and Pugh, Ronnie. "Hillbilly music," *Grove Music Online. Oxford Music Online.* (Accessed 22 July 2008) <http://www.oxfordmusiconline.com>

[105] "Humphrey, Mark. "What is Old-Time Music?" *The Old Time Music Home Page.* (Accessed 21 July 2008) <http://www.oldtimemusic.com/otdef.html>

[106] Tribe, Ivan M. "Country Music," *Grove Music Online. Oxford Music Online.* (Accessed 24 Jul. 2008) <http://www.oxfordmusiconline.com>

[107] Malone, Bill C. "Western swing," *The New Grove Dictionary of Jazz*, 2nd ed., ed. Barry Kernfeld. *Grove Music Online. Oxford Music Online*, (Accessed July 25, 2008) <http://www.oxfordmusiconline.com>

[108] Smithers, Aaron. "What is Western Swing Fiddling?" *Texas Folklife Resources: Study Guide—Western Swing.* (Accessed 21 July 2008) <http://web.archive.org/web/20020816131707/http://www.main.org/tfr/sg_swing.htm>

[109] Zenger, Dixie Robison. *Violin Techniques and Traditions Useful in Identifying and Playing North American Fiddle Styles.* D.M.A. dissertation, Stanford University, 1980.

[110] "Fiddling," *Encyclopedia of Music in Canada; The Canadian Encyclopedia.* (Accessed 21 July 2008) <http://www.thecanadianencyclopedia.com/index.cfm?PgNm=TCE&Params=U1ARTU0001206>

[111] Graham, Glenn. *Cape Breton fiddle music: The making and maintenance of a tradition.* M.A. thesis, Saint Mary's University, Canada: 2004.

[112] Carr, Kevin. "Quebecois fiddling," *Strings.* July 2001, Vol. 16, 1: 28-29.

[113] "Who Are the Métis?" *Métis National Council.* (Accessed 21 July 2008) <http://www.metisnation.ca/who/index.html>

[114] "Traditional Metis Music And Dance," *Metis Culture & Heritage Resource Centre Inc.* (Accessed 21 July 2008) <http://www.metisresourcecentre.mb.ca/history/music.htm>

[115] Surette, David. "The British Aisles," *Strings.* Nov.-Dec. 2003, Vol. 8, 4: 84-89.

[116] Cranitch, Matt. *The Irish Fiddle Book: The Art of Traditional Fiddle Playing* Cork, Ireland: 2001.

[117] Bjorndal, Arne. "The Hardanger Fiddle: The Tradition, Music Forms and Style," *Journal of the International Folk Music Council*, Vol. 8. 1956: 13-15.

[118] Neal, Mary Elizabeth. *Devil's instrument, national instrument: The Hardanger fiddle as metaphor of experience in the creation and negotiation of cultural identity in Norway.* Ph.D. dissertation, Indiana University, 1991.

[119] Vollsnes, Arvid O. et al. "Norway," *Grove Music Online. Oxford Music Online.* (Accessed 23 Jul. 2008) <http://www.oxfordmusiconline.com>

[120] Bohlin, Folke et al. "Sweden," *Grove Music Online. Oxford Music Online.* (Accessed 23 Jul. 2008) <http://www.oxfordmusiconline.com>

[121] Brashers, Bart. "A Brief History of the Nyckelharpa," *The American Nyckelharpa Association.* (Accessed 23 July 2008) <http://www.nyckelharpa.org/resources/history.html>

[122] Fredelius, Gunnar. "Nyckelharpa," *Grove Music Online. Oxford Music Online.* (Accessed 23 Jul. 2008) <http://www.oxfordmusiconline.com>

[123] Norbeck, Henrik. *Swedish Traditional Music.* (Accessed 21 July 2008) <http://www.norbeck.nu/swedtrad/index.html>

[124] Rosén, Anders. "The Nyckelharpa," *Hurv.* (Accessed 24 July 2008) <http://www.hurv.com/english/articles/nyckelharpa/nyckelharpa-eng.htm>

[125] Rosén, Anders, "The Orsa style in perspective," *Hurv.* (Accessed 24 July 2008) <http://www.hurv.com/english/articles/orsa/orsa-style-eng.htm>

[126] "What is a Nyckelharpa?" *The American Nyckelharpa Association* (Accessed 23 July 2008) <http://www.nyckelharpa.org/resources/index.html>

[127] Martin, Christine. *Traditional Scottish Fiddling.* Isle of Skye: Scotland, 2002.

[128] Burford, Freda and Daye, Anne. "Contredanse," *Grove Music Online. Oxford Music Online.* (Accessed 23 Jul. 2008) <http://www.oxfordmusiconline.com>

[129] "Hornpipe." *Oxford Dictionary of Musical Terms.* ed. Alison Latham. New York: Oxford University Press, 2004. 86.

[130] Dean-Smith, Margaret. "Hornpipe," *The New Grove Dictionary of Music and Musicians.* ed. Stanley Sadie. London: Macmillan, 1980. 8:721.

[131] Collinson, Francis. "Reel," *Grove Music Online. Oxford Music Online.*(Accessed 24 Jul. 2008) <http://www.oxfordmusiconline.com>

[132] Tilmouth, Michael, and Lamb, Andrew. "Schottische," *Grove Music Online. Oxford Music Online.* (Accessed 17 Aug. 2008) <http://www.oxfordmusiconline.com>

[133] "Strathspey," *The Oxford Dictionary of Music.* ed. Michael Kennedy. *Oxford Music Online.* (Accessed 22 Jul. 2008) <http://www.oxfordmusiconline.com>

[134] Collinson, Francis. "Strathspey," *Grove Music Online. Oxford Music Online.* (Accessed 22 Jul. 2008) <http://www.oxfordmusiconline.com>

[135] Kuntz, Andrew. "Bile Them Cabbage Down," *The Fiddler's Companion.* (Accessed 21 July 2008) http://www.ibiblio.org/fiddlers/BI_BILE.htm#BILE_THEM_CABBAGE_DOWN

[136] Kuntz, Andrew. "Devil's Dream," *The Fiddler's Companion.* (Accessed 21 July 2008) <http://www.ibiblio.org/fiddlers/DEV_DHU.htm#DEVIL'S_DREAM_[1]

[137] Kuntz, Andrew. "Irish Washerwoman," *The Fiddler's Companion.* (Accessed 30 May 2007) <http://www.ibiblio.org/fiddlers/IP_IZ.htm#IRISH_WASHERWOMAN>

[138] Gammond, Peter. "Ragtime," *The Oxford Companion to Music.* ed. Alison Latham. (Accessed 27 Jul. 2008) *Oxford Music Online* <http://www.oxfordmusiconline.com>

[139] Hitchcock, H. Wiley, and Norton, Pauline. "Cakewalk," *Grove Music Online. Oxford Music Online.* (Accessed 28 Jul. 2008) <http://www.oxfordmusiconline.com>

[140] Berlin, Edward A. "Ragtime," *Grove Music Online. Oxford Music Online.* (Accessed 25 Jul. 2008) <http://www.oxfordmusiconline.com>

[141] Berlin, Edward A. "Scott Joplin," *Grove Music Online. Oxford Music Online.* (Accessed 28 Jul. 2008) <http://www.oxfordmusiconline.com>

[142] Bordman, Gerald and Hischak, Thomas S. "Irving Berlin," *Grove Music Online. Oxford Music Online.* (Accessed 25 Jul. 2008) <http://www.oxfordmusiconline.com>

[143] "One-step," *Grove Music Online. Oxford Music Online.* (Accessed 27 Jul. 2008) <http://www.oxfordmusiconline.com

[144] Badger, Reid. "James Reese Europe," *Grove Music Online. Oxford Music Online.* (Accessed 29 Jul. 2008) <http://www.oxfordmusiconline.com>

[145] Badger, R. Reid. "James Reese Europe and the Prehistory of Jazz," *American Music,* Vol. 7, No. 1, Special Jazz Issue. Spring, 1989: 48-67.

[146] Tucker, Mark, and Jackson, Travis A. "Jazz," *Grove Music Online. Oxford Music Online.* (Accessed 29 Jul. 2008) <http://www.oxfordmusiconline.com>

[147] Evans, David. "W.C. Handy," *Grove Music Online. Oxford Music Online.* (Accessed 25 Jul. 2008) <http://www.oxfordmusiconline.com>

[148] Steinblatt, Jim. "The Handy Man Can," *ASCAP Playback Magazine.* Oct.-Dec. 1998. (Accessed 30 July 2008) http://www.ascap.com/playback/1998/october/handy.html

FIGURE NOTES

Fig. 1.1 Angel with Renaissance fiddle. Melozzo da Forlì, c.1478-80. Pinacoteca, Vatican Museum, cat. 40269.14.5. From a fresco created for the choir of the church of the Apostles in Rome. Although the original fresco was destroyed in 1711, some of the figures such as this one were detached and saved and are currently housed in the Vatican in Rome.

Fig. 1.2 Picture of Rebec. Agricola, Martin. *Musica instrumentalis.* 1528.

Fig. 1.3 "Columba Aspexit," fragment of musical manuscript from Hildegard of Bingen's *Rupertsberger Riesenkodex*, 1180-1190. Wiesbaden, Hessiche Landesbibliothek, f. 476.

Fig. 1.4 Heavenly citizens of Jerusalem playing musical instruments, from Hildegard of Bingen's "Liber Divinorum Operum," *Lucca Codex*, 1240.

Fig. 1.5 Illustration of the Violin Family. Praetorius, Michael. *Syntagma Musicum*, vol. 2. Wolfenbuttel, 1619.

Fig. 1.6 Fingerboard and scale from Robert Crome's *The Fiddle New Model'd, or a Useful Introduction for the Violin, Exemplify'd with Familiar Dialogues.* London: J. Tyther, c. 1740.

Fig. 1.7 "Minuet in C" from Robert Crome's *The Fiddle New Model'd, or a Useful Introduction for the Violin, Exemplify'd with Familiar Dialogues.* London: J. Tyther, c. 1740.

Fig. 2.1 An unknown Venetian 18th century violinist and composer, often mistaken as Antonio Vivaldi. Anonymous painter, Museum of Music, Bologna, Italy.

Fig. 2.2 *The Thames and the City.* Oil by Giovanni Antonio Canal, known as Canaletto, 1746-47. National Gallery, Prague.

Fig. 2.3 *Antonio Vivaldi.* Engraving by James Caldwall, c. 1725 (in imitation of François Morellon La Cave's 1725 engraving). This engraving was used by Sir John Hawkins as an illustration in his 1776 publication *A General History of the Science and Practice of Music*: 839.

Fig. 2.4 *Johann Sebastian Bach* at the age of 63. Portrait by Elias Gottlob Haussmann, 1748.

Fig. 2.5 *George Frideric Handel.* Oil painting by Balthasar Denner, 1726-8.

Fig. 3.1 Mozart with his father Leopold and his sister Marie Anne. Watercolor by Louis Carmontelle, 1764.

Fig. 3.2 *Schubertiade at the home of Josef von Spaun.* Sepia drawing by Moritz von Schwind, 1895.

Fig. 3.3 *The Palace of Esterhaza.* Painting by Bartolomeo Gaetano Pesci, 1780.

Fig. 3.4 *Portrait of Beethoven.* Photograph of a reproduction of a painting by Carl Jaeger (1833-1887). Library of Congress: LC-USZ62-29499.

Fig. 4.1 *Sigr. Paganini.* Daniel Maclise, 1831.

Fig. 4.2 *Hardanger Fiddle Scroll.*

Fig. 4.3 *Pauline Garcia-Viardot.* Lithograph by Déveria.

Fig. 4.4 Felix directing a home musicale while Fanny sits watching. Illustration from a Victorian biography.

Fig. 4.5 *The Madeleine.* Photograph of the famous Parisian church, the Madeleine.

Fig. 4.6 *Jules Massenet.* Photograph of the French composer, Massenet (1842-1912).

Fig. 4.7 *Carmen.* Poster by L. Leray for the first run of *Carmen* at the Opéra-Comique, Paris, 1875.

Fig. 5.1 *The Violin.* Oil on three-ply panel by Juan Gris, 1917.

Fig. 5.2 *Stravinsky.* George Grantham Bain Collection, Library of Congress: LC-B2- 5464-2.

Fig. 5.3 *Maurice Ravel,* photograph from Calvocoressi, M.D. "Maurice Ravel," *The Musical Times.* Dec. 1, 1913.

Fig. 5.4 *Béla Bartók.* signed high school graduation photograph, 1899.

Fig. 6.1 *Galaxy of Musicians.* Oil by Raja Ravi Varma (1848-1896).

Fig. 6.2 *Erhu, Chinese folk instrument.*

Fig. 6.3 *Fiddlin' Bill Hensley, a famous old-time fiddler.* Asheville, North Carolina. Photograph by Ben Shahn. Library of Congress: LC-USF33-006258-M3.

Fig. 6.4 *The Ragtime Violin.* Cover from *The Ragtime Violin* sheet music, composed by Irving Berlin, and published in 1911 by Ted Snyder Co., New York.

Fig. 6.5 *The Castle Walk.* Cover from *The Castle Walk* sheet music, composed by published in 1913 by Joseph W. Stern & Company, New York. Vernon and Irene Castle are shown on the front cover, dancing.

www.ingramcontent.com/pod-product-compliance
Lightning Source LLC
LaVergne TN
LVHW081316060426
835509LV00015B/1544